A Pocket History of
GAELIC CULTURE

AL⋯ITLEY

THE O'BRIEN PRESS
DUBLIN

First published 2000 by The O'Brien Press Ltd.,
20 Victoria Road, Dublin 6, Ireland.
Tel. +353 1 4923333; Fax. +353 1 4922777
e-mail books@obrien.ie
website www.obrien.ie

ISBN: 0-86278-569-3

British Library Cataloguing-in-Publication Data
Titley, Alan,
A Pocket History of Gaelic Culture
1.Civilisation, Celtic 2.Celtic Music - Ireland 3.Irish literature -
Ireland
4.Art, Irish 5.Ireland - Civilisation
I.Title II.Gaelic Culture
700.9'415

1 2 3 4 5 6 7 8 9 10
00 01 02 03 04 05 06

The O'Brien Press receives
assistance from

The Arts Council
An Chomhairle Ealaíon

Layout, editing, design: The O'Brien Press Ltd.
Maps: Design Image
Cover separations: C&A Print Services
Printing: Cox & Wyman Ltd.

INTRODUCTION

The terms 'Gaelic' and 'Culture' in the title of this work are notoriously elusive and impossible to define. 'Culture' is certainly one of the most difficult words to which a controlled meaning can be assigned in any Western language. It raises up notions of the totality of a way of life on the one hand, and the more confined sense of the arts of music, sculpture and literature on the other. Beyond that we sense that it may have something to do with the cultivation of turnips and mangles, or with the possession of a well-stocked mind replete with a sensitive knowledge of Beethoven and Bach, of Rodin and Racine. If 'Culture' does not quite mean anything we want it to mean (like Lewis Carroll's Humpty Dumpty), it is certainly a loose and shaggy monster shaking its locks.

'Gaelic' is equally messy. It appears to refer to a language which is spoken in Ireland, Scotland and the Isle of Man, but has offshoots in the games of hurling and Irish football, and in a kind of coffee made with whiskey, sugar and cream. In a bad English pronunciation with loss of post-vocalic 'r' it may sound like a kind of vegetable which keeps vampires at tooth's length. 'Gaelic society' generally refers to Irish society before we were defeated in the wars of English expansion which began with the Tudors in the late sixteenth century.

Its use in English is quite new, however. It is no more than a crude anglicisation of the Irish word *Gaeilge* (the Irish language), or the adjective derived from it, *Gaelach*, which refers to the human activities characteristic of the society in which Irish was the chief spoken language. You can see that we already begin to bog down.

For the purposes of this book 'Gaelic' will refer to the cultural dynamics which found their origins and inspirations in the native tradition of Ireland (while admitting that 'native tradition' is a problem of meaning and reference in itself). The language will be referred to as

'Irish' throughout. This is because it is the historically correct usage for the native language of Ireland, and the word 'Gaelic' is often commandeered by people who wish to suggest that the relationship of the Irish language to the country was somehow peripheral, or belonging to a disaffected and cranky minority. There is the added difficulty that 'Gaelic' is now commonly used to describe the Celtic language of Scotland, and despite their shared history down to a few short hundred years ago the historically native languages of Ireland and of Scotland are not now mutually intelligible. In fact, 'Irish' was the word given to both languages by linguistic and imperial authorities until the seventeenth century. The term 'Gaelic' with incorrect reference to the Irish language in Ireland is little more than a hundred years old.

Most students in Ireland are taught Irish in schools and colleges until the end of their required education. Visitors to the country will hear their friendly Aer Lingus pilot or air hostess greeting them in a language which they do not know. Even non-perceptive travellers will notice placenames and signs on public buildings in a kind of recognisable English and in another tongue which bears little resemblance to the common stuff of European directions. Yet when they open their ears they will hear hardly anything except the common English which has been sweeping the over-developed and not-so-developed world for the last hundred years. Whatever difficulty they may have with this is less likely to be caused by the substratum of Irish on which Hiberno-English used to be based, than by the strangulated vowels and decapitated consonants which are the hallmark of the new urban middle-class speech of the filthy-rich Irish.

The Irish learned in school is sometimes excellent, sometimes indifferent, and sometimes appalling. The Irish spoken in the remaining Irish-speaking districts can be replete with historical and living plenitude, or alternatively riddled with English words and idioms. Many Irish students have spent some time in these Irish-speaking areas known as *Gaeltachtaí*. Yet, many Irish people are totally ignorant of how or why these areas exist, what their relation is to the rest of the country, why it is that they are required to learn the language at school, how come that for most of our history everybody in the country spoke it and nothing else and that we now generally speak English. Visitors are puzzled by the ghostly traces and passing wisps of this strange language which they encounter in public life, and which from time to time they tune in to on radio and televison or in the chance eavesdropping of a street corner. Ireland, at once apparently almost entirely English-speaking, and yet so different in its cultural make-up from the stuffy formality of British middle-class life and so hugely outside the straight-jacket of mainstream European class-culture, remains an enigma and an oasis.

This book addresses these enigmas and answers them. It explains clearly where the Irish language has come from and where it is, what its relation to Gaelic society is, what that Gaelic society might be, the nature and extent of literature in the Irish language, the 'native' elements in the music and dance which we now enjoy, and the extent to which 'Gaelic' culture still lives and thrives in Irish life.

English versions of Irish words are given except in the case of phrases of common usage; words in Irish are generally given in their modern form. Translations of poetry/verse are by the author.

BEGINNINGS

When the languages of the Earth were scattered after the tower of Babel was destroyed by the wrath of God, the great linguist Fénius the Ancient was the only one to remember each and every one of them. In the passage of time he gave this knowledge unto his grandson who made the Irish language out of the shards and bits of the 72 tongues which he had inherited. In this way, the Irish language was the very essence and distillation of the first tongue of the earth which God gave unto mankind. This grandson, named Gael Glas, lived peacefully in Egypt while the Israelites were kept in captivity by the nasty bastard Pharo and his imperial swine. In due course these descendants of Gael Glas – consequently colloquially known as *Gaeil* or Gaels – were also driven out without benefit of manna or the leadership of Moses and spent years of tribulation in Scythia. Thence they did high tail it west into the Mediterranean and conquered Spain. All this time they were developing the intricacies of the early Irish verb which both trained their minds for the literature they were about to compose and passed the time before the invention of crosswords and dancing.

On a clear afternoon in winter one of these people climbed up a tower which his tribe had built and looked to the north. Far away he saw an island fringed with green sward and bedecked with deer-filled forests and surrounded by salmon-leaping seas, and he looked again and he saw that it was good. An isle of the blest set in a mist-filled sea. This distant prospect and aspect most sublime inspired the Gaels to prepare for an invasion of that new land. Having conquered Spain they must have presumed it would be a doddle. It was not thus or so. On a fine morning with a fair wind behind them they set forth in mud-caked coracles up the Bay of Biscay, past the Gaulish coast, across St George's Channel (which it was not then), until they found what they were looking for.

Three attempts it took before they gained a successful landfall and managed to butcher some of the inhabitants. The first try was at Derry where the native population, the *Tuatha Dé Danann* (the People of the Goddess Danu), copped on quickly and decided to do the invaders in as soon as they had a look at them. The second attempt was near Kenmare in Kerry and resulted in several disasters. One of the leaders fell off a mast and cracked his skull. Another rowed ahead of his companions but lost his oar and was drowned. When they eventually struck the shore their poet Amergin – whose wife had also been drowned during the invasion (although this did not inhibit him) – burst into poetry:

I am the wind scouring the foam
I am a breaker of the sea
I am the growl of the ocean
I am a roaring bull
I am a hawk on the cusp
I am the sun through the dew
I am the salmon which leaps
I am the wonder of art
I am the spear which wins the battle
I am the wild boar of courage
I am the pool of plenty
I am the ken of knowledge
I am the god who seized the fire of creation.
Who gives meaning to the light from the sun?
Who can confabulate the age of the moon?
Who can read the secrets of the tree?
(If it is not me?)

This damburst of creativity is sometimes entitled 'The Mystery' which is entirely appropriate as nobody has the least clue what it means. On the one hand it seems to be the voice of the conqueror claiming the land for his people. On the other, the pride of the poet who can create anything at all he likes out of the wonder of his own head.

After their landfall, they made some headway tricking the people of Kerry into compliance but were eventually prevailed upon to return to their ships. Once there, the druids of the *Tuatha Dé Danann* raised a great storm and blew them back to sea. In the first act of poetic humility (not often emulated), Amergin, who had already claimed the country for his own, had another go and concocted a verse which calmed the waters. This allowed them to travel as far as the Boyne estuary and the rich Meath muck and to grab as much of the good land as they could. After a fierce battle, they crushed the *Tuatha Dé Danann* at Teltown, which forced the defeated to go underground and live in the land of the fairies. From then on the country was theirs and they could do with it as they liked. That is how the Gaels, or the Irish, came to Ireland around 333 BC.

The perceptive may have noticed that this is utter tosh. It is, of course, a summarised version of the Irish telling of their own history. Every nation is entitled to its own version of its story, but its own version is not necessarily true. It is true, of course, in the sense that this is the version that the Irish accepted for themselves for about 1000 years and which validated their identity. It sustained them when they were being rubbished by imperialist historians in the sixteenth and the seventeenth centuries, and it gave them a tale on which they could hang their hats. Elements of it are still accepted by serious scholars who strive to unravel the blurred rays of the dawn of Irish history.

The ghost of this story lives in the standard version of how the Irish language – and therefore, Irish society – came to Ireland, according to Celtic scholarship. That version invokes the notion of there being a great grouping of Celtic peoples roaming the forests and steppes of Europe from the Dnestr to the Duoro, fashioning the same pots and dipping their ladles into the same cauldrons. They must have come out of the crotch of Indo-European society over a thousand years before Christ was crucified and rambled into eastern Europe before the Roman Empire set its greedy paws upon that region. The Celts spread across the continent depositing their gods in Vienna and Lyon, and their shards and their spear-tips wherever archaeologists might choose to dig. Some quite hundreds of years before Christ groups of them who could not pronounce their 'q's and had turned them into 'p's crossed to what is now Britain and populated a relatively deserted land, and some generations later other groups landed in what is now Ireland, bringing primitive prehistoric proto-Irish raw-in-tooth-and-jaw with them. That is to say, the Irish language and the society which it supported was an import – although a very early import – brought here by a recognisable bunch of ethnically aware pirates and adventurers whom we call the Celts.

There are some problems with this version, most of which are scholarly.

The first of these has to do with the very notion of the 'Celts' themselves. 'Celtic' can mean (a) a 'racial' grouping like the Semites, or the Slavs, or the native Australians; (b) a style of art or pots or decorative elaboration which was commonly found in central Europe and is sometimes associated with La Tène culture; (c) a language family with certain shared grammatical features.

These meanings do not coalesce or coincide.

In recent years the problem has been compounded because of the proliferation of massive charlatanry in the guise of Celtic spirituality and Celtic healing and Celtic cookery and Celtic coffee-table culture. With regard to (a) above, it is difficult to lend any clearwater credence to racial theories based on blood and guts and phrenology. In the case of (b) it is plain that material artefacts travel more easily than ideological or religious ones do. If I drive a Mitsubishi car and we are all blown away by a neutron bomb it would not be correct for a future archaeologist to conclude I was Japanese. Language families (c) are handy designations to link structurally similar speech codes together, but no other conclusions can be drawn from this. The majority of Peruvians now speak Castilian but they are most determinedly not Spanish; nor are Brazilians Portuguese nor Berbers Arabs. Apart from a strictly defined linguistic term, we would be well advised when we hear the word 'Celtic' to go for our crap-detectors.

A different scenario entirely is painted by the archaeologists whose discipline may be seen as rag-and-bone stuff by linguists and historians. They are at one in insisting that there is no evidence whatsoever for any large-scale invasion of the country in the first millennium BC. If a new warrior class had arrived in this period and conquered the native inhabitants, imposing their language and their way of life on them, it would be highly probable that such an invasion would show itself in the archaeological record. In fact, it would be certain. No such record exists. They conclude, therefore, that the 'Celticity' of Ireland – whatever that might be – goes back a long, long way. They further conclude that the Irish language is *not* an import, but most likely grew and developed on the island over a much longer period than the 2500 years of which we normally speak. It is a beguiling proposition.

There is, of course, the further question of Irish art. Although not amenable to easily defined characteristics, historians of early Irish art would tend to agree that there is a continuity of style and shape and imagination between the first manifestations of decorative art some thousands of years BC and the art of the Irish Golden Age after the coming of Christianity. We can easily acknowledge that the Book of Durrow or the Book of Kells or the leaky Ardagh Chalice belong to Gaelic culture. Because of the theory of the Celtic invasion we are less inclined to see the Petrie Crown or the Clones dress-clasp, which predates it, as part of the same story. But Irish art is a continuum from its beginnings to the great ruption of the seventeenth century. The decorative stones outside Newgrange may just as well be part of Gaelic material culture as the harp of Brian Boru. In fact, if the idea of a 'cumulative Celticity' is true, then the language which the builders of Newgrange spoke during their mead-breaks might well be described as a kind of precursory anterior forespoken seedling protoprior primitive Irish.

EARLY SOCIETY AND MYTHOLOGY

There was a rich native Irish tradition before the coming of Christianity in the early fifth century. The preChristian may well be longer in terms of actual years than the Christian which now seems to be drawing to a close. But without historical records we can only speculate as to its actual nature and content.

It is impossible to recreate Irish pagan religion out of the shards and bits that have been left to us. It may not even have been an organised religion with its own hierarchy of gods such as the Classical or the Egyptian worlds possessed. Religion demands an Olympus where the gods live, with numerous subgods farmed out performing their delegated functions. But we do not have any temples to these great gods, or scrolls of their rules and threats.

Irish pagan religion only lives in the mythological stories which have come down to us in the ink of Christian quills. We have neither a pantheon nor a theology. But these stories may be more real than any attempted reconstruction. People think richly in stories before they become reduced to the thin gruel of organised dogma. The stories *were* the religion and there is no need to go beyond them.

When we do so we are led into seeming anarchy and

chaos. We dimly discern a great god, *Eochaidh Ollathair*, 'the father of all' or the *Dagda* as he was more commonly known. He was, at once, crude, coarse and all-powerful and in some depictions was ugly and gross. Unfortunately, we also possess an equally powerful god by name of *Lug*, or *Lugh Lámhfhada*, who was seen as a master craftsman and a patron of the great skills of fighting, music, poetry, history and magic. Ths *Lug* left his name as a Celtic God in Lyon – formerly Lugdunum – and Leyden and Carlisle and even in London, if speculative etymology is to be believed. Some memory of him survived in the harvest festival of August or *Lughnasa*, which contains his name. Other gods presided over knowledge, the brewing of beer, smithwork and bloodsucking. They could be wise and comforting or gross and ridiculous. Goddesses also did abound and were especially associated with fertility. One of the names given to the gods of preChristian Ireland is the *Tuatha Dé Danann*, the 'People of the Goddess Danu', and Danu (or Anu) herself pops up in placenames. Other goddesses such as Brighid or Macha were variously related to the gods by mate or by marriage. Put simply, Irish religion was an 'earth-religion' looking down to the fertility of the land, whereas Christianity might be seen as a 'sky-religion' where the ultimate truths resided somewhere over the rainbow way up high.

There was an Irish Otherworld, but it was not a place where the souls of the saved or the damned went after death. It was a world which lived side by side with the common and everyday world, but in a different dimension. It was a world interwoven with our own that people could move in or out of on special or unusual occasions. It was a world which survived in folk belief down to the present day in stories of the *sí*, or the fairies. Christianity may have been triumphant but it never quite eradicated the remnants of the ancient religion which kept on changing and re-ordering itself over 1500 years.

All of our knowledge of the Irish deities comes from our stories. They have their history also. Irish mythology tells of the battles of the *Tuatha Dé Danann* against a race of demons whom they ultimately vanquished. They were in turn conquered by the Gaelic Celts when they came to colonise the country. The defeated gods retired underground to live in mounds and cairns and caves and holes, to become the fairies of later folk tradition.

Defeated gods when they are not completely killed off become at first heroes and later mere mortals. Many of the Irish mythological stories reflect the confusion between man and god in a time when magic seemed commonplace and the supernatural was part of everyday life. The story of Mír and Éadaoin is one of those beautiful tales which is more twilight than Celtic. Éadaoin, the beautiful young woman who falls in love with Mír, is turned into a pool of water by Mír's jealous wife. The pool changed into a worm which in turn became a butterfly which followed Mír, everywhere. He knew that it was Éadaoin and that she loved him. She was blown away by the wind and spent many years in misery, although she was also protected in a special sun-bower by a friend. The jealous wife pursued her and attempted to drown her in a drink which belonged to the woman of a warrior. She quaffed her drink and became pregnant, and thus Éadaoin was born for the second time. Needless to say herself and Mír got together again and lived happily ever after.

But we get very little of this misty atmosphere in the great epic of pagan Ireland, the *Táin Bó Cuailnge* or 'The Cattle-Raid of Cooley'. It is the great epic because of its length and breadth and complication; it is pagan because, despite being saved and redacted by Christian scholars in Christian times, there is no hint of that Christian world of clerics and grace and God's will and salvation and heaven above. We can be sure that it reflects something of the spirit of the times and the stuff of the imagination before the coming of Patrick.

The story itself is fairly simple. Maeve, the queen of Connacht, one tough woman, has a row with her husband over which of them is the richest. When she discovers that all she is lacking is a bull as good as his, she sets about acquiring the best there is in the province of Ulster. As the owner does not want to sell it or give it up she turns to war. Ulster is defended by the hero Cú Chulainn who has to stand alone for most of the invasion because of a weakness that has afflicted the army. This he does successfully by valour, heroism, trickery, intelligence and magic. Despite his best efforts, however, the Connacht army manages to sneak away with the bull and return home. Maeve's newly acquired bull defeats her husband's in a head-to-head contest, and leaves the defeated animal's guts and innards strewn all over the countryside. The queen's gloating was short-lived, however, as the Brown Bull of Cuailnge decided to up and away back home after his gory victory.

It may be asked what is so remarkable about this epic. There does not appear to be anything uplifting about it, no great moral, nothing that helps us understand human emotion and conduct. It is rambling, diffuse and inchoate, even in its better versions. And yet, there is a great power in its telling and some unforgettable set-pieces which stand out for their force and individuality in Irish literature. Cú Chulainn himself is an inspiring figure in his heroism, his frailty, even his self-doubt. The descriptions of his spasms when he becomes possessed by anger and the spirit of war are exuberantly grotesque. His single combat with his friend Ferdia is moving and tragic. His struggles with the phantom Morrigan show us the easy intervention of gods in the ways of men. There may be the shadow of dynastic conflict behind the epic but its principal value, after the story itself, must be the glimpse it gives us of the aristocratic and therefore barbaric values of that preChristian world on which so much of Irish culture sits. It is also worth noting that the *Táin* is composed in prose. There are some poetic toenails ingrown through the narrative but its medium is description and talk. A prose epic is quite unusual from the dawn of literature but it is a measure of how much Irish culture had advanced that it has already left behind the jerky breathing of early poetry when we meet it right at the start.

Early Irish society is generally described as tribal. This is particularly unhelpful as the words 'tribe' and 'tribal' can be used to denote a large nation of tens of millions of people in parts of Africa, or the yowlings of the followers of the Kilkenny hurling team. In prehistoric Ireland it can only mean that loose alliances of small groups of people who lived in proximity to one another joined together under a common name against other loose alliances of other small groups of people who lived some distance away. When we consider that when Patrick came to Ireland there may have been no more than 200,000 people in the entire country from wood to wood, we get a clearer picture of what is meant by a tribe. Most of them lived on coasts or riversides or lake edges. The country was thickly covered with dense forest run fiercely wild.

The social units are generally described as *tuatha*, which literally means 'peoples', but which we can usefully translate as 'states', 'political communities' or even 'petty kingdoms'. Kings were common. Society was hierarchical as societies with more than one person usually are. The kings and their households and their learned toadies – including their poets – were the aristocracy. Below them were those people skilled in more specialised crafts, particularly smiths of all kinds. Below them again were the freemen, clients of some lord or other, in possession of land or permission to use it. Beyond these were various classes of tenants. At the very bottom were the truly unfree

– serfs and slaves and bondspeople. There was nothing very communal about this society, and it was certainly not democratic. Even though the name of a territory is usually given as relating to a chieftain or king, it does not mean that the ordinary people were in any way descended from him. We can be sure that when ownership of land changed and one expanding dynasty crushed another with axes and adzes, the ordinary people went about their business with bent backs and an eye to the nearest bush. Even a change in religion probably did not make a huge change in their lot.

CHRISTIANITY

The very first date we can be sure of in Irish history is AD 431. In this year Pope Celestine sent a bishop by the name of Palladius to Ireland to minister to the Irish who already believed in Christ. This may have had something to do with the crushing of the Pelagian heresy which denied original sin and taught that man could be saved by his own offices. One contemporary writer tells us that Pelagius himself was Irish, which is an interesting twist and showing that no sooner had some Irish become converted to Christianity than they immediately began inventing heresies of their own. Although Palladius has been largely written out of history it is probable that he played a large part in re-establishing orthodoxy and in consolidating a Christianity which altered Irish Gaelic culture permanently. There is an alternative theory that Palladius never arrived at all – the documentation speaks of him as being sent – or that he was swiftly put to the axe after arriving in the country as a riposte to his meek-and-mild stuff about love and brotherhood.

Whatever the truth about Palladius, the story of Patrick is a lot more sexy. This is partly because we know so much more about him, and partly because so much more still has been embroidered around him. He is exceptional in being the only person from the fifth century to have been captured as a slave, to have escaped, and to have lived to write about it. Although the primary purpose of his *Confession* is to defend himself against his detractors and enemies (of whom he had many) there is some autobiographical material in it. It is here that we learn of his capture at the age of 16 by Irish slavetraders, his menial work for six years tending hogs and sheep on a mountain, his escape after a long and arduous trek, and his being called back in a dream by the people of Ireland.

Beyond that we begin to juggle the pieces. We do not have any dates for him. It seems more likely now that he came here in the second half of the fifth century, perhaps in AD 456 and continued on for nearly 40 years. He was a Romanised Briton, probably from North-Western England, whose family was involved with the Church, his grandfather having been a priest. His mission to Ireland was entirely a personal affair. He was a kind of freelance preacher who went his own way and did his own thing without any official sanction. This unorthodox wheeling and dealing did not endear him to either the Irish aristocracy who were rightly suspicious of him as he was about to blow their world away, or the more right-thinking clerics always suspicious of the visionary and uncontrollable. We know he was accused of making use of his position to line his purse, and his own strenuous denials only emphasise the seriousness of the charge.

Whatever the truth of it he was spectacularly successful. Or if he was not successful, his biographers, hagiographers and cult-followers finished the job for him. As early as the first half of the seventh century we have praise poems in his honour. Later in the same century we have the first biography in Irish, but obviously drawn from earlier sources. It is in these early works that we first encounter the fanciful stories about him, particularly his magical contests with the druids. The legend of Patrick banishing the snakes from Ireland is a much later one, probably from the twelfth century. Other stories from the early tradition, although quite mad, contain an ironic truth. We are told that when he was baptising king Aonghus at Cashel he drove the spike of his crozier through the foot of the unfortunate royal. Patrick noticed nothing until after the ceremony, probably when he tried to retrieve his stick with a plop. When he asked him why he did not complain the king replied that he thought that suffering and torment were part of the ceremony. Patrick was duly impressed with his understanding of the tenets of the faith.

The story of Patrick and its environs illuminate several aspects of Irish culture at this time.

In the first instance Irish society was in an expansionist phase in the first half of the fifth century. Patrick tells us of thousands of slaves who were captured in Britain and made to sweat it out in Ireland. Irish raids on Britain may have intensified after the withdrawal of the Roman legions in AD 410, but it is also likely that their attacks weakened the rotting empire in the west and speeded its downfall. It was at this time that the Irish began to move into Scotland across the northeast coast of Ireland to establish a kingdom with a recognisably Gaelic form which was to last for 800 years. There were also Irish colonies in Wales and in southwest England, but these never grew into any lasting organised polity.

The conversion of Ireland was not effected easily. When Patrick himself speaks of the non-Christian gods he speaks with a venom of which only the righteous are capable. This is over and beyond the power and personality evident in the rest of his writings. Crushing the druids and smashing their idols may be legend, but it bespeaks a struggle between two ways of life which must have lasted for some hundreds of years. The High King of

Ireland, Diarmaid Mac Cearbhaill, who lived in the middle of the sixth century, was still unconverted to Christianity. Stories grew up around his tussles with various saints and which are only one example of a whole strand of literature which reflects the clash between the old paganism and the fashionable new cosmopolitan religion.

THE *FIANNAÍOCHT*

One of the devices which the inventors of Irish literature used to bridge the gap between the old and the new was to imagine a debate between those who lived in pagan times and the Christians themselves. They took one of the characters from the *Fianna,* or Fenian, stories and poems and brought him forward in time by an ingenious piece of science fiction to when Patrick stalked the Earth. The *Fianna* were a band of warriors whose business it was to defend Ireland in pagan times, although, as with NATO, we are never told who they are meant to be defending it against. In reality, if there was a reality, they were more than likely a bunch of testosterone-laden lads who were banished from their communities during those years when wild oats are mostly sown. Their leader was *Fionn mac Cumhaill* whose name was spelt *Find* or *Finn* in earlier renditions.

Like other heroes Fionn may originally have been a god and some scholars suggest that his name is embedded in the city of Vienna when his writ ran around Europe. He was both warrior and visionary, however, and many tales tell of his visits to the magical Otherworld. He was said to have the power of seeing the future by sucking his thumb. This gift was variously explained by the fact that he once got his hand stuck in a door leading into the Otherworld, and only his thumb stayed inside; or that he was the first to taste of the Salmon of Knowledge whose flesh gave the gift of prophecy. Although this thumb-sucking hero was renowned for his martial prowess and nobility, Irish literature does not hesitate to equally describe him as a jealous cad, a vindictive swine and a dirty old man.

The stories and poetry which grew up around Fionn and the Fianna are probably an invention of the twelfth century and onwards. But they do reflect an underlying reality of tension between the Christian clergy and the ordinary people or their representatives which goes back a long way. Fionn's son Oisín fell in love with a beautiful woman from the Otherworld. She brought him to *Tír na nÓg* or the Land of Youth where people stayed forever young without benefit of work-outs or cosmetic surgery. After 300 years in their love-pad, Oisín thought that he would like to visit his people again. He was granted this wish on condition that he never set foot on the soil of Ireland, but stayed on his fine white steed. Despite the disadvantages of performing all human functions from the back of a horse, he agreed. He had not realised, of course, that 300 years had gone by since he had left, and was duly surprised to find his people dead and scattered and St Patrick doing his rounds converting people and chastising druids.

This narrative trick is the ideal vehicle for the debate which ensues between Oisín and Patrick. We are not surprised when Oisín is given all the best lines and delivers all the best arguments:

> Hey! Patrick, you blather away
> And raise your crozier to strike,
> Your crook would be smashed to bits
> If my son Oscar could fight
> Yourself or your three-leafed God
> Here, now, face to face
> And you thrashed him fair and square
> I'd admit you had a case.

Oisín became fashionable again during the Romantic

movement because of the forgeries of the Scottish writer James MacPherson under the anglicised spelling *Ossian*. Even then, people were willing to be fooled by Celtic charlatanry. His son Oscar gave his name to the great Irish playwright and wit Oscar Wilde through his parents' interest in legend, mythology and the Irish language.

By the way, Oisín eventually died because he bent down to help an old man lift a stone and fell off his horse. He didn't die because of the fall, however, but by instantaneously growing 300 years older on touching the ground.

WRITING

Apart from the religion itself the single most vital result of the missions of Palladius, Patrick and their peers was the introduction of writing. It is true that there was a kind of writing being used for some restricted purposes since the fourth century. This writing was known as *ogham* and was enacted by carving notches and strokes along a vertical line on stone or on wood. More than 300 stones with ogham engravings on them survive in Ireland, Scotland, the Isle of Man, Wales, Cornwall and even in England. They were erected to commemorate people as we find only the names of deceased persons on them, sometimes with a mention of their 'tribe'. We never find a trace of Christian symbolism, and they are always written in primitive Irish of a kind which was probably archaic even when they were being written.

The tradition tells us that this writing was invented by the god *Ogma*, an Irish deity of poetry, knowledge, wisdom and music. It is more likely it was put together by the learned classes who had begun some tangential acquaintance with Latin on which the ogham script is based.

Latin made a direct impact with the Christian mission. It is said that Patrick himself instructed people in 'alphabets', that is, in writing. We can assume that it took quite some time for this strange new way of committing sounds to symbols to take root. In the first instance, the Irish clergy were being instructed in Latin, which was a language they never heard spoken. However bad British Latin was, at least it had been used as the speech of the occupying armies within living memory. And if later French is anything to go by, the Latin spoken in Gaul must have been weird indeed.

Some time during the late fifth or early sixth centuries the new Irish learned class – Christian, monkish and monasteried – began the task of fashioning their own tongue into Roman letters. This had its own particular difficulties. Irish is a language whose sound changes at the beginning of words (among other places). It was essential to invent a system that would show this change without losing the root letter. There are classes of slender and broad consonants in Irish which don't exist in Latin. Irish vowels can be long or short. They managed to solve most of these difficulties and commit the language to writing in a standardised norm from the very beginning.

Equally extraordinary was the script they used. Although obviously derived from some kind of contemporary Roman model, the script the Irish developed was entirely their own. It is sometimes called 'insular script' because the Irish exported it to England and Scotland during the next hundred years; but it was never used outside the islands of Ireland and Britain. This form of writing is often seen as a 'missing link' between earlier and later Latin script. The Irish also introduced new conventions such as capital letters, spaces between words and elements of punctuation. While these were initially introduced into Irish writing in Latin, they appear at the very beginning of Irish literature properly so called. That is to say, stories, poems, sagas, rhetoric in the Irish language with a long antecedence which finally began to be written down on parchment and vellum and the hides of beasts.

EARLY IRISH LITERATURE AND ART

Whatever other claims we may like to make about Irish literature it *is* the oldest continuous unbroken vernacular literature in Europe with the single exception of Greek.

Oldest, of course, does not mean best or most wonderful in whatever sense these comparative terms can be applied to literature. But it is remarkable and worthy of necessary repetition.

This literature began to be written down in the monasteries – we must presume – from the mid-sixth century onwards. A date of around AD 565 is given for a poem entitled *Luin oc elaib* ('Birds compared with swans') which is said to have been composed by Colmán mac Lénéni, a contemporary of St Columba. A different scholar gives the interesting word *focricci* as the very first Irish word we can be sure of in a manuscript at the end of the sixth century. Although the monasteries were thoroughly Christian we have to imagine some kind of compromise with the native secular schools of learning which had neither gone away nor been totally assimilated. We also have to think of a monastery, not as an entirely holy place, but as a centre of commerce and political activity. In fact, a monastery was a town, and in particular, a university town.

Each monastery had its scriptorium, usually a separate building devoted to the writing of books, just as there were buildings for the making of pots and pans, or for the safe storage of slaughtered beeves. These books were the holy books of scripture lovingly transcribed and decorated by specialist scribes. The glories of the Book of Kells or the more unfortunate Book of Durrow (dipped in a trough by a Midlands farmer for many years, to ward off disease in cattle) are well-known products of these scriptoria.

The same kinds of authors and scribes who brought us these wonderful examples of illuminated art also brought us early Irish literature. The quills that once painted Christ in all his glory in inks imported from the Mediterranean or from Asia Minor for a decorative gospel manuscript also scratched out early redactions of the *Táin Bó Cuailnge* or the first glimmerings of the story of Mad Sweeney, *Suibhne Geilt*, in carefully crafted letters.

Early Gaelic culture was all of a piece.

Across the yard from the silversmith working painstakingly on the Ardagh Chalice may have been a writer of fevered imagination writing a voyage tale or a personal lyric. The craftsman who designed and created the Tara Brooch might drop in for a chat with the composer of an *Eachtra* or a *Toghail*.

If the 'island of saints and scholars' has a romantic ring to it when referring to this Golden Age of art and literature, it does have a basis in lived reality. Modern sensibilities may be more wary of the saints than of the scholars, but the central concept will not bear knocking.

The twin careers of the near contemporaries Columbanus and Colm Cille, also known as Columba, illustrate the learning, the sainthood and the literature. Columbanus is generally associated with the reconversion of Europe. He travelled extensively through Gaul, Switzerland and Italy founding monastic houses in the late sixth century. When a dispute arose with local bishops he appealed directly to the Pope in Rome. He wrote a learned and clear Latin which shows a strong and dominant personality.

Colm Cille, on the other hand, went north to Scotland and founded the famous religious settlement of Iona. His prestige and his alliance with the Irish kings of Dál Riada led largely to the conversion and gaelicisation of Scotland with a bible in one hand and whatever passed for a claymore in the other. Later tradition, which may be largely based on fact, paints him as a man of great energy with organisational ability, determination and learning. He founded monasteries in Ireland and was in continual touch with them, even though one story tells that when he went to Scotland as a pilgrim for Christ in expiation for his sins, he swore he would never walk on Irish soil again. Folk wisdom came around this problem by having him return with Scottish clods under his feet. One of these return journeys was to the great meeting of Druim Ceat where he prevented the poets from being banished from Ireland because of their overweening arrogance by a neat compromise which reduced their numbers (but that was more than 1500 years ago).

Other stories have him subduing the Lough Ness monster, having direct communication with angels, and his birth and death being accompanied by supernatural marvels. Whatever about those, it does appear that he did compose poetry and hymns, and one of the earliest poems we have in Irish was composed on his death. The O'Donnells of Donegal carried the *Cathach* of Colm Cille into battle with them – a copy of the hymns said to have been written by him and encased in a special cover which still exists – until the early seventeenth century, but the fact that they didn't always win argues against its authenticity. The Book of Kells, however, is the product of his own monastery of Iona and a visible manifestation of the power and prestige of Gaelic culture at its strongest.

Although Colm Cille was deeply involved with the world, there was a different strain within the Irish Church which saw that it would best praise God in the isolation of the margins of places. This hermetic movement is best illustrated by a place such as Skellig Michael, a rocky promontory soaring high out of the waves off the coast of south-west Kerry. Here a handful of monks scraped out a precarious life glorifying God between the crashing of seas and the squawking of gannets. It was in such isolated communities that some of the freshest Irish poetry was composed. It was nature poetry done because it was felt along the heart and not for gain or profit. It was done because nature is a manifestation of God's beauty and deserves to be celebrated. Much of this poetry was never read by anyone until the twentieth century, although we can be sure that much more of it was written down. This quatrain, for example, was scribbled hastily between other duties because the writer was struck by the beauty of the music of a bird:

The lark is the lord of music
I stand at my cell and hear
him spill such wonder from his beak
where God's sky is blue and clear.

No matter how striking or beautiful these may be to our sensibility they are not representative of the larger body of old Irish literature. Much of the poetry was purely a practical matter, not because the Irish were particularly poetic, but because verse is more easily committed to memory than prose. We have poems on the geography of the country, for example, or the history of the world. Long boring poems containing the names of kings. Poetry in praise of chieftains and petty tyrants. But we have strikingly significant religious poetry, at least in the extent of its ambition. The *Féilire Aonghusa* ('The Calendar of Aongus'), for example, runs to more than 2000 lines in fairly strict metre. The subject matter is not exactly riveting, naming as it does the saints who were remembered on every day of the year, but literature at its best also has a direct grasp of life and is not just an airy extra. Even more ambitious is *Saltair na Rann* ('The Psaltar of the Verses') whose line-count tots up at more than 8000. It is a retelling of the bible story in poetry but with an Irish flavour.

Similarly, we have a lot more early Irish prose of a functional rather than a purely aesthetic nature – if that division can be maintained. We have annals, history, lives of saints, genealogies, sermons, visions, laws and lore of places as well as the heroic stories of gods and bulls and wooings and slaughter. The sheer volume of early Irish literature is itself remarkable. There may be as much as 5000 pages of text available to us, and this takes no account of what was utterly destroyed in the course of time. These texts include myths and sagas, biblical glosses, laws, lives and martyrdoms of saints, names of persons and places, poetry, hymns and politico-religious propaganda. The laws alone have been edited in six fat volumes amounting to 2353 pages or more than a million words, and are a mine of information about early Irish society and the early legal mind.

Irish law was, of course, heavily influenced by Christianity and even though there was a class of 'native' *breithiúin* or judges, it seems that the laws themselves may have been first written down by learned churchmen. We have specific legal texts dealing with contracts, robbery, marriage, property, the professions, the obligations of judges and others which all seem very modern. Texts on lunatics, idiots and the insane, or on class and rank show us that not much has changed. Laws dealing with satire, bees, deer, cats, dogs, trees, sport and wounding point us to specific aspects of early Irish society.

Some of these laws appear eminently sensible to modernity and must have made exciting court cases. A woman could divorce a man if he was impotent or was too fat to practise intercourse. It might have been interesting to see what evidence was produced in these kinds of cases. Some punishments are reasonably novel to us such as allowing people to die of starvation in a hole or setting them adrift on the sea in an offshore wind without a paddle. If God wished them to return, then they would. But if not, then ... Robbery was often punished by the chopping off of a hand but nowhere are we told what happens in the case of a successful appeal. Rape could be punished by castration, and if the victim became pregnant the rapist had to bear responsibility for the rearing of the child. We cannot pretend that things were great for women despite a few enlightened shafts. One legal aphorism speaks of the three darknesses into which women should not go: 'the darkness of mist, the darkness of a wood, and the darkness of night'.

What we have in early Irish society is a culture confident in itself, a bright light on the dark edge of Europe, a glory that was not Rome. The eminent historian Toynbee speaks of this society as one with the possibilities to become a great civilisation. It was a possibility that aborted.

IRRUPTIONS

On the margin of a manuscript a monk of the ninth century penned these four lines:

Is acher in gáith innocht
fo-fuasna fairggae findfolt.
Ni ágor réimm mora minn
dond láechraid lainn ua Lothlind

Tonight the savage wind rips
the white hair off the sea;
In such a vicious storm as this
the Viking pirates can't threaten me.

The implication is obvious. A new and deadly ingredient had been added to the Irish brew. Although the annals can often be a litany of births, pillages and deaths, there is a sense of society settling down in the closing years of the eighth century. Readers of horoscopes and portends of disaster of that time should have copped on that something was afoot in 788 when the moon appeared to turn to blood. Although the Irish were well used to inter-dynastic strife and the normal barbarities of rural society, there must have been something particularly frightening about the first Viking attack on Rathlin Island (off the Antrim coast) in 795. It was unexpected and unprecedented. In the same year other islands were attacked off the west coast. It might be that these were the same raiding party circumnavigating part of the country and sussing it out. At the same time Colm Cille's beloved island of Iona was attacked by Vikings on their way south. It was attacked again on several occasions in the early years of the ninth century, culminating in the massacre of 68 people in the year 806. This forced the community to retreat to their monastery in Kells, bringing their famous book with them. The Book of Kells would properly be called the Book of Iona were it not for the Vikings.

This removal is itself symbolic of the disruption that the Viking raiders visited upon Irish society and culture.

After this things hotted up. Within 20 years they had grown from being hit-and-run, get-in get-out quick plunderers to wintering big fleets on Irish rivers. In 837 we learn of fleets of 60 ships on the Liffey and the Boyne. This probably meant about 3000 men in each case, a fighting force able to contest political power with most kings. One author speaks of 'great sea-vomiting of ships'. Their attacks spread out along the rivers through the midlands. They then set up naval settlements or *Longphoirt* (hence the town and county of Longford), some of which became permanent and the basis for organised town life.

There is a picture of the Viking raids embedded in the public consciousness, which is not entirely true. The notion of axe-wielding pirates jumping off long ships and slashing the local population is undoubtedly factual (although they never wore those two-horned helmets), but it is likely that they left the greater part of Irish society untouched. The reason we know so much about them is that they raided the monasteries. They raided the monasteries because these were the centres of commerce and of riches. The histories were written in the monasteries by the very class of people who suffered most by the actions of the Vikings. In every revolution some people win and some people lose and some people don't figure at all. Most people did not suffer by the Viking raids, and settlements and large areas of Gaelic culture remained untouched by their depredations.

Attacks by Irish monasteries on one another were a lot more common than the worst that the Vikings could do. But what made the Vikings different was that they were outsiders who spoke a different language and to the Irish had a barbaric religion. When, for example, in 807 the monasteries of Clonfert and Cork went into battle with one another, resulting in much slaughter and bloodshed, the Irish were able to fit it into the normal pattern of intercommunal strife. When a fleet of 60 Viking ships appeared on the Liffey in 837, however, it must have terrified the local Dubliners who knew not whence they came nor what was in store for themselves. It is because of their foreignness and exotic presence rather than their immediate domination that the Vikings figure largely in the Irish story.

After the initial series of raids the new invaders began to settle down, organising towns in what proved to be more geographically useful areas than the Irish monastery towns. Thus Dublin grew from being a small dung-ridden Irish mud settlement on one bank of the Liffey to being a bigger dung-ridden clay-and-wattle Viking settlement on the other. Likewise they organised themselves in fortified pockets alongside the local Irish in Limerick, Cork and Waterford until assimilation through intermarriage, familiarity and mutual respect quickly set in. For the first time we see placenames appearing and taking root which are not of Irish Gaelic origin. Although in Dublin they used one version of the Irish *Dub linn* (the black pool) in place of the more commonly accepted Irish one *Áth Cliath* (the ford of the sticks), *Veigsfjorthr* (Wexford) and *Vethrafjorthr* (Waterford) take their place alongside the Irish *Loch Garman* and *Port Láirge*.

Apart from these placename deposits – Scandinavian blobs left pat on an Irish countryside – their continuing legacy was thin enough. Their influence on Irish literature may be confined to the introduction of a theme, and this appears after the Vikings themselves had been well and truly thrashed. They appear by name in some of the stories about Fionn mac Cumhaill and the Fianna where Ireland is defended by its heroes against the ravages of outsiders from *Lochlann*, the Irish word for Scandinavia. Anachronism never bothered a good story, for we even find them being introduced into some of the mythological stories about prehistoric Ireland. What this means is that the Vikings become a type of the marauding outsider in Irish literature and are used whenever an enemy is required. Even less prominent is any influence of Norse literature itself on Irish writing. Irish syllabic poetry was well established when the Vikings first arrived and whatever their own forms of verse may have been they seem not to have brought them with them when they came here. This may be quite simply that pirate adventurers and greedy merchants are not the most fruitful bearers of high culture.

Their physical impact did, however, cause some changes in the Irish language. The Vikings introduced many words to do with shipping and shopping that exist in Irish today. The Irish word for boat, *bád*, is a Scandinavian borrowing superseding but not obliterating the established word *long*. *Margadh*, a market, lived alongside the native *aonach*, although they began to take on slightly divergent meanings. It is always dangerous to suppose that the lack of a word in a language denotes the lack of the object or the concept referred to. However, the Scandinavian *pingin* or penny was certainly novel to the Irish, even though it appears that, having introduced coinage to the country, the Vikings then quickly forgot about it.

It may be that their contribution to Irish society in the long run was more as traders and as entrepeneurs than as freebooting marauders. When the Irish seized Limerick from them in 968 the Vikings took away a great store of valuable golden and silver artefacts and richly embroidered fancy clothes, which can only have come from Europe or from farther east. Their cosmopolitan connections leavened Irish culture and opened a window on the world.

The leavening was not all one way of course. A large part of the Irish cultural diaspora in the ninth and tenth centuries was as a result of scholars and learned men fleeing from Viking terror. The drowning of books at home meant that they were brought to the continent for study and safekeeping, and there is some irony that the quote on page 29 was discovered in the margins of a manuscript in the library of the monastery of St Gall in Switzerland. The Irish contribution to European culture at this time was significant. Almost alone, they kept Latin learning alive, developed the art of writing, and were the intellectual mainstay of a troubled Christian Church.

According to tradition Viking power in Ireland was crushed at the battle of Clontarf, fought just outside Dublin on Good Friday 1014. On the one hand there stood the Irish forces under the leadership of the High King Brian Boru and on the other the massed ranks of the Vikings under some nameless leader. After a ferocious battle which lasted from the break of day to the dying of the light the foreigners were driven into the sea, scrambling into their longboats to make the dispirited journey back to Stavanger or some lonely fjord. The reality is a bit more mixed and much more mundane. Although it certainly was an important battle, the power of the Norsemen had waned by that time, or they were just another force within the Irish political system. The battle was occasioned by the provincial king of Leinster revolting against Brian Boru's rule and enlisting the Dublin Vikings on his side. Brian had the help of the Limerick and Waterford Vikings, so that it was much more a battle between Munster and Leinster than between native and coloniser. It was Brian's literary dynasty which fashioned the battle into the great story it was to become, a story which constantly gathered bits and accretions until at least the eighteenth century.

This great Gaelic myth did have some truth to it. Brian was a great king, if we mean by a great king somebody who kills off more of his opponents than they do of his kind. He was a great military commander, a patron of the arts, a friend of the church (putting his relations into important ecclesiastical positions) and an astute propagandist. He became the type of the great Irish High King for hundreds of years after his death and remained a symbol of Gaelic power and prestige for generations.

Nor was this symbol without some reality. It can be argued that the political power and stability of the Irish-speaking peoples was never greater than after the battle of Clontarf in 1014, and after the battle of Carham on the Tweed four years later when the Scottish King Malcolm consolidated his rule over all of Scotland.

Irish was spoken from Mizen Head in the south of Ireland to John o'Groats in the north of Scotland, from the Aran Islands in the west to Buchan Ness in the east.

Whatever happened within this large area was Gaelic culture in whatever sense of that word we choose to mind.

It was a confident culture open to the world on its own terms, refashioning its own literature, building its material base, expanding trade with continental Europe, evolving native and cosmopolitan learning, and involving itself with the normal petty dynastic squabbles of political power. It was a situation which began to unravel in Scotland quite quickly after the murder of the great Scottish King, Macbeth – much maligned as a conscience-stricken, wife-beaten, ghostseeing soothsucker by Shakespeare – in 1057. In Ireland, the squeeze began with the Anglo-Norman expedition of 1169, and although of little enough consequence in itself, managed to establish a bridgehead for the involvement of English power in the affairs of Gaelic Ireland. The rest of the story of Gaelic culture is largely a tale of a culture in conflict with this power.

THE ENGLISH INVASION

Historians are divided as to what the couple of hundred mercenaries who landed in a sandy creek in Co Wexford in May 1169 should be termed. They are variously called Normans, Anglo-Normans, Norman-French, Norman-Welsh and less savoury names. There is little doubt about what they called themselves, or what name the Irish had for them. The contemporary Irish said they were *Saxain*, that is to say, English, and this is what they normally used for themselves. For that reason, even though many of them spoke the French of the English aristocracy or the Welsh of Pembroke, it is most accurate to speak of them as English.

The reason and the occasion of their coming is a great story of power and betrayal and sex and adventure, but is largely irrelevant as it is certain that they, or others like them, would have come anyway. Proposals for an English conquest of Ireland were discussed at a royal council at Winchester in 1155, and permission was sought from the English Pope, Adrian IV, to undertake an invasion of the country in order to bring the native church under the control of Canterbury. The Pope duly wrote his letter authorising the action. It was not acted upon, however, until the deposed King of Leinster, Dermot Mac Murrough, sought help from the English King, Henry II, to regain his titles and his land. Henry gave him permission to recruit mercenaries in his own territories, and Dermot consequently hooked up with a gang of greedy opportunists. The most famous of these was Richard Fitz Gilbert, later known as Strongbow, a dissident landholder whose power had been much clipped by Henry. Dermot promised him some fat land in Leinster and the less fat hand of his daughter Aoife in marriage. Strongbow obliged, but we do not know what Aoife thought of the bargain.

The result was a series of incursions of adventurer

English lords, partly under the control of Dermot Mac Murrough, but increasingly doing their own thing. Because of their growing independence of everybody, Henry himself came to Ireland with a significant army in October 1171 and stayed for nearly seven months. His object was to ensure that his freebooting adventurers did not become strong enough to challenge his authority. Royalty at that time did not have the mystique that it has today after years of diets of fairy tales and tabloid slaverings. Kings and princes were more likely to be seen as holders of power by the spilling of plenty of blood than as personages whose veins ran with that especially thick product known as royal blood. The result of his successful campaign of harrowing and ravaging was that the English crown began a permanent interest in Ireland, an interest sometimes matched by an Irish befixedness with the English crown. One of the ironies of this settling of English speakers in Ireland is that Henry himself spoke no English at all, although he did have some understanding of it.

As with the Vikings, it would be wrong to speak of an English or Anglo-Norman *conquest* of Ireland. They made enormous confiscations in less than a hundred years. Many of the Irish chiefs and lords were dispossessed in Leinster and in east Ulster. But the main effects were largely peaceful. Unlike other campaigns there were very few pitched battles between the Irish and the invaders. Where there were, the Irish were as likely to be as successful as their enemies even against fortifications and walled towns. The fine English castles from the twelfth and thirteenth centuries which we still see around the country were halls of residence and administration more than defensive structures to keep the braying natives at bay. The point of the English involvement in the late twelfth century was that it provided small islands of English power in an ocean of Gaelic Irish culture. These islands never vanished completely, making their presence a defining mark in Irish history. They were used to bring in English serfs and vassals, along with their hangers-on and doxies and ecclesiastical carpetbaggers. Despite the fact that they were squeezed and hung out to dry and hugely diminished within three generations, they remained a *permanent* presence. Hence their importance.

GAELIC CULTURAL AREA IN
MEDIEVAL/MODERN TIMES

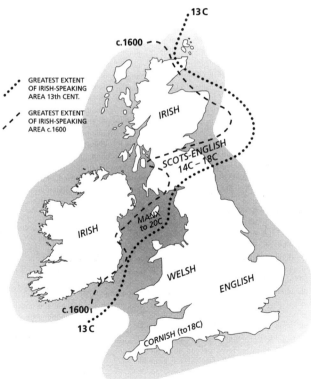

• • • • GREATEST EXTENT
OF IRISH-SPEAKING
AREA 13th CENT.

✓ ✓ ✓ GREATEST EXTENT
OF IRISH-SPEAKING
AREA c.1600

13 C

c.1600

IRISH

SCOTS-ENGLISH 14C – 18C

MANX to 20C

IRISH

WELSH

ENGLISH

c.1600

13 C

CORNISH (to 18C)

THE SCOTTISH CONNECTION

When does this story start, who really knows?
Nine thousand years ago will do we may suppose,
but give or take a thousand here or there
seven thousand and three BC or some such year
Some blokes with unknown speech and tongue
in coracles caked with mud and crap and dung
crossed west some water which no one yet had
    named
and to more boring virgin land they came
sans history, *sans* past, *sans* anything that can be
    construed
as identity, and all that baggage which we now renew
each year as St Patrick milks the course
or Billy rides upon his whitened horse.
In those times no one really gave a damn
For all that only mattered was who could man
a boat or plough or fought to save the tribe
or carved out other reasons to survive.
Millenia on when fortune had much improved
and names and things began to stick like glue
(what else?) some others with labels, like, let's say,
    Scots
went back across the water, got a toe hold, first
in Galloway, Argyle, round about the Mull of Kintyre
where mist rolls in from the sea, and where they
    conspired
to set up a kingdom, Dál Riada, which now is
    attached
to housing estates in Dublin's more salubrious parts
but not quite as fancy yet as Tudor Court, as Windsor
    Lawns,
(and definitely not Jacobin Lane or Jacobite Downs?)
Irony insists they were just returning home

but those before them watching on the shore
with painted bodies whom history now calls Picts
had reason to be suspicious of warriors bearing gifts
of smiles and blander and some new-fashed faith
about a god who died and rose and whom now they
ate.
Colonists tend to bring high god-talk on their sea
which blur distinctions between invader and invadee.
Thus these Picts or natives, call them what you like,
succumbed to market forces, to axe, to sword, to
Christ
And like their painted bodies scoured with Scottish
rain
left history's stage to tougher, violent, that is,
cultured men.
These were our guys, in this our only expansionist
phase,
just as skilled, no doubt, in the ways of death and
how to raze
a hamlet here, a homestead there, in rape and pillage
and cutting throats – you know the stuff – the
common coinage
of armies on the march and the baggage in their train:
doxies, farmers, chancers, sayers of sooth and even
saints.
Colm Cille was not, of course, your average saint at all
son of a king, or whatever passed for that, in
northwest Donegal,
more likely a fat cowherd with some marts to spare
who wished a church education on his son and heir
never dreaming that the call 'Thy Kingdom Come'
would mean that his own kingdom came undone.
But his own son, the Dove of Derry, didn't have to
think

how Christ and Caesar always interlink
because on this Earth there is no more powerful
    brew
than that which politics and religion together do
    construe.
So when to Scotland with his twelve disciples did set
    forth
and settled in Iona, it became monastery and court
and centre for propagation and for spreading wide
Ireland's one and only colony beyond the tide.
We gave them our language, Irish, later Scottish,
    sometimes Erse
and fashioned it to their own desires, for better or for
    worse.
They call it Gallick now, a neutral term which serves
    to fake
its origins, or its embarrassing past to obliterate.
Like calling French *francayse* or German *Dutch*
or Spanish *Pisspaniol* or some such
transmogrification of historic truth
being ignorant and obfuscating just to boot.
We named their country, from one of our own gods,
    Scotia
and named their landscape, southeast to northwest all
    over
as a tourist's glance at a tourists' map must show
topography will always live in the afterglow
of the naming namers, those whom like the gods
    create
a world from nothing, and inscribe upon it their eyes,
    their fate,
their wonder, their joy at this their world being young
the first note humming for all their songs being sung.
Ni hannsa, non dificile, we can set it out in lines

the harmonious intermingling through the rings of
    time:
Ben Nevis, Binn Éadair, Ben Dearg, Ben Gulban,
    Loch Ness
with or without a monster, Killarney, Kilmarnock,
    Long Kesh,
Lough Neagh, Loch Lomond, Lough Conn, Loch
    Rannoch, Lough Flesk,
Glen Fiddich, Glen Rovers, Glen Gregor, Glen
    Domhain, Glen Esk,
Dundonald, Dunfermline, Dundalk, Dundee, been
    there, done that,
Dunblane, Dunmanway, Dún Éidin, Dungarvan,
    Mountrath,
Montrose, Mountmellick, Greenock, Greencastle,
    the Aran Isles,
Arran off the coast of Ayr, and Burtonport, the Isle of
    Skye,
The isle of Inishfree, north sea oil, and Kinsale gas,
Kintyre, Kinsealy, Kingussie, Kincasla, Wester Ross,
Rostrevor, Rosinver, Rosscarbery, and onomastics too,
MacNeill, McCarthy, MacLeod, McGurk, MacPhee,
    MacHugh,
MacDonald, Mac Dómhnaill, Daniels, Donaldson,
    O'Donnell,
Cambery, Cameron, Cambden, Callum, Camman,
    Campbell.
The point does not need labouring that our cultures
    intersect
on the ship of history, from topmost rigging to the
    lowest deck
and if the cruel hand, of whom we wish to blame, did
    not intervene
the shape, the cut, the thrust, the map, the entire (as
    we now say) scene

would be entirely different, but that's the way it
    goes;
you win some and you lose some in the magic history
    show.
There was, of course, Duns Scotus, you recall our £5
    note
the Irish philosopher, looking miserable under his
    hairy cloak
against the German winter, or maybe he had a hint
that his students were going to kill him for the crime
    of making them think.
And then a further example, the case of one MacBeth
that Scottish king, who in Shakespeare's play was put
    to death
by this guy Malcolm, son of a previous king, one
    Duncan one
who is painted as a goodie, but if the truth be known
was a fairly nasty piece of work, who was not averse
to spiking babies in their cradles, and maybe what
    was worse
poisoning in time-honoured medieval fashion, those
who might be rivals, opponents, pretenders, or who
    chose
to open their big mouths. Typical totalitarian stuff
but this in itself was never quite enough
to make historians back off in their normal rush to
    judge
or more importantly, world-famous dramatists to
    fudge
the difference, between the truth of a person's
    reputation
and what was then expedient in a given situation.
Certainly easier to lick King James's butt
than biographical lies to resoundingly refute.
It was said that Shakespeare always loved a lord

true or not, he could certainly not afford
to buck the toadies around King James's arse
like dingleberries dancing in a farce.
For Shakespeare was, no more than others, a great
    revisionist
rewriting stories, reshaping facts, as any dramatist
will do for sake of story, of theatrical impact
and in that case, who cares for, those things called
    facts?
The truth is MacBeth is not at all as he appears
he reigned quite peacefully for more than seventeen
    years
and when he was cruelly murdered in AD 1057
he left a country which had been at peace
for a generation plus, which is more than we can say
for others, those Irish-Scottish kings who had their
    day,
and from whom he sprung in a direct line of descent,
kings of Dál Riada, *a mbarúil*, the brightest in the
    firmament.
But those of us who are republicans don't give a fuck
we prefer to see all kings' heads on the block.
And when I say republican, I crave the literal sense,
I mean intelligent, those who know what it means,
    not the dense
tabloid-drugged, Murdoch-moroned, TV-zonked,
    abair, fools
who wouldn't know what's cop-on from a rule.
Wisdom for us is ten thousand Diana jokes
and happiness each time a prince or sultan croaks.
We love the tales that show that royalty's not as bad
at those who slobber and salivate as their names are
    sad.
The greatest king who e're in England reigned

was Charles the first of whom it could be claimed
was full six feet tall when he took the throne in 1625
but was reduced to five feet six at the very time he
    died.
But it was his forefathers dumped the hero of
    Shakespeare's play
MacBeth Mac Findlaech Mac Ruairidh, Mormaer of
    Moray
and ushered in a line of craven and rotten Stuarts
thus the play that bears his name was produced first
    in court
before James the first of England, but of Scottish
    Jameses sixth
whose purposes then were political, as much as if
artistic, and insists again be read
more carefully than the bald account of Holinshed.
MacBeth, then, as Scottish as a Scottish night is long
who spoke nothing but his own first native Irish
    tongue
For though other kings spoke Irish down to James
    the fourth
It never was again chief language of the court
for when Birnam wood did come to Dunsinane
the English thing took root, the Irish waned.
The English Queen called Margaret it was began
the rot, with southern ways and customs and land
grants to solid reliable burghers of English speech
which pushed the Gaelic language on its long retreat.
For this her good work Margaret was later canonised
In matters of politics and culture is God really
    non-aligned?
This, then was the first great cultural fissure
which religion and politics deepened, but did not
    quite sever

the deep connections (sometimes also merely
    sentimental wail)
between what later writers loved to dub 'the
    sea-divided Gael'.
There were times, we must aver, they fully paid us
    back
in cultural exchange, not just the Gaelic origins of the
    Big Mac,
or Scotch whiskey, or post-match feeds of cans of
    Tennents lager,
or that more recent Glasgow import, Mars Bars
    dipped in batter.
(We slipped them too the occasional pig in a poke
like the bagpipes – they haven't yet quite seen the
    joke!)
There was John Carswell, the Presbyterian divine,
    who took
responsibility for writing and publishing the very first
    book
ever printed in Irish between solid hard covers
his version of Calvin's *Book of Common Order*
in Edinburgh in 1567. In his preface he addressed
the people of Scotland and of Ireland together, and
    impressed
upon them the word of God according to Calvin, and
    their need
for instruction in their common tongue being sprung
    from common seed.
For perfectly valid reasons, about one hundred years
    ago, they
had occasion to raise his earthly body from the clay
and discovered a giant of a man, full seven feet tall
whose body from top to toe had not decayed at all
which only goes to prove, if proof were sought
that those who write in Irish are beloved of God;

or else, or yet, this other seems more right
that what they lack in fame, they gain in height.
Though Carswell put dour Calvin's creed in glossy
    Irish words
the Irish themselves were not seduced, although
    more ensured
by politics, by distance, by interdynastic strife
than any firmly held beliefs on death, on life.
And yet, I doubt, if we could ever embrace
a creed which banished life's laughter from the
    face
and although we had our share too of po-faced
    prelates
I doubt if many of them were quite as zealous
as that minister on Skye who, to take no chance
banned sex, in case it would lead to dance.
Language, though, for all its selfsaid power can not
    escape
the weightier crush of matters, both church and state,
so when that Scottish James, to whom we did refer
decided that his rebellious Ulster subjects would
    never
again threaten the safety of his crown or line
his final solution he with pomp unveiled in 1609.
Good solid burghers and land-hungry farmers he
    resolved to send
across to Ulster, and take the Irish from their homes
    and land;
this policy with such success he did pursue
that the killing fields it started we still renew.
So when Ewings kicked out Farrells, or Lennons
    were overrun
by Forsythes, or the Nesbitts took the castle of
    Cathal MacElgunn

it seemed so distant in the past, far away, and long
ago
but the battle fought four centuries since is what is
still fought now.
Scottish civil warfare and Scottish uncivil strife
still chew our cud of memory, still demand
bloodprice
for dark deeds done for whatever reason and without
regret
in the time and clime of Duncan's son, and his queen
Margaret.
So when you are accosted upon the street after
another Celtic disaster
and you know full well what those thugs from hell,
just what it is they're after
to know that you're from Rangers too, or at least just
anti-Catholic,
But you cop on, and say, come on, 'I'm from Thistle
Partick.'
'Scotland is the name of what you call Ireland,'
Robert Louis
Stevenson's Catríona told her David Balfour, but he
was only
expressing the patently obvious, that no cultural
atlas's faultlines
can hope to read, or adjudicate between the minds
across the short hop from Catholic Spain to Muslim
Morocco
or the shorter jaunt from Burgerland to the South
Texan town of El Paso.
In Europe itself, without much search, great
differences can be found
between villages which guzzle wine, and others
which resound
with the clink of beerglasses, somewhere along the

fiftieth parallel

which also divides, as football buffs full know, the
predictable

plodding football method of teams out of the frozen
north

from the silken skill and Latin thrills of those who
are not short

of excitement, imagination, daring, wonder, those
from sunny lands

who know that soccer is not really Gaelic football
without hands.

But then culture takes on shapes and cuts and thinks
and forms

Configurations of desire we take as universal norms.

Most of us here are familiar with Phil Larkin's clever
quip

the one made with some regret, but in a flip-

pant tone, that 'sexual intercourse began in 1963

between the end of the Chatterley ban and the
Beatles first LP'.

Seismic change does not come like this, wrapped up
and neatly planned

We cannot, then, as John Major once said, draw a line
under the sand

and assert the crucial date is 1969, or 1974, or 1922

or further back, 1609, 1690, depending on your point
of view.

It's worse than this, and deeper than our easiest
theological dispute

for white Christian, mostly English-speaking people
the roots

of conflict go beyond debate of virgin birth or
predestination

and find their springs and sustenance in the nature of
imagination

for Irish and Scots are of common stock
call them Paddys, Teuchters, Biddys, Jocks
and a little more generosity, a smidgen more of
    reason
might bind the wounds first opened up by bishops
    and by Calvin
and beyond that too a bridge of sighs that all of us
    must cross
between the left bank of old popery and the right
    one of John Knox.
But none of this prescinds at all from the horror of
    what happened
Scotland's history racked and torn, savagely
    misshapen
by, well, let's call a spade a spade, or a claymore
a useless tool against cannon and a smallbore
gun: an imperialist adventure, an expansionist
    campaign
into the unknown north of Britain, and on a rain
filled day in April 1746, at Culloden, upon Drumossie
    Moor
the army of two poxy princes fought, one the
    Hanover whore
of Babylon, the Duke of Cumberland from whose
    savagery and greed
they named the flower 'Sweet William', but to the
    Scots just a weed
called 'Stinking Billy', because they had their own
    hero, the royal Scot
young Bonnie Prince Charlie, much less a leader and
    more of a sot.
'Change princes and we will fight you again!' but it
    would no' matter
the war brought two ways of life, two wells from out
    the past together

One army moulded by the discipline of whip and
lash

the other a raggle-taggle of fractious clansmen who
did not fash

to choose a decent ground. Five hundred yards of
brackish bog across a closing mist

where the Irish-Scottish union and twelve hundred
years were lost.

What followed was the normal triumphant dance of
victory

when civil laws and order straighten out barbarity.

In Inverness just one day after the necessary
slaughter

the streets were swept for the very first time of dung
and ordure

and triumphant soldiers were brought to book and
even sent away

for the heinous crime against God and kirk of looting
on a Sunday.

5'5" in his stockinged feet was the average
Cumberland soldier

the five feet most important in the battle, the five
inches after

as they raped and plundered across the land reducing
bonny banks

and braes and glens to a desert where miserable
survivors gave thanks

that they amongst the few lived to taste the culture
shock

of firelocks turning self-belief into the tugging of
forelocks.

Nor was that enough, they soon easily learned how
human life was cheap

Within a hundred years their lands were cleared and
they exchanged for sheep.

So when Wordsworth's highland lass did sing an air
    sweet and slow
of half-forgotten far-off things and battles long ago
it was, more likely, a present song of hurt and loss
    and pain
of things locked within her spirit then, but would
    ne'er be out again.
After that then it was just downhill all the way
a famine here, a clearance there, Burns suppers, St
    Patrick's day
Simian Paddies out of Punch, and similar Scottish
    captions
'Are you a mechanic?' said the cartoon, 'No, I'm a
    McPherson.'
Kilts and haggis, aran sweaters, *ól agus craic*
compensatory symbols of genuine loss, of what we
    lack
deep within ourselves, in the heart's most keenly felt
emotions, or affirmation of Arnold's binary
    'imaginative Celt'
and 'practical Anglo-Saxon.' Who knows? I merely ask
and hope that we are equal to the task
of binding up what history has torn apart
with the real rag and bone crops of our art.
Some years ago, Sam Thompson, the Ulster poet
(his name reveals his background) wrote
'I love my native land, no doubt/
attached to her through thick and thin.
Yet though I'm Irish all without/
I'm every item Scotch within.'
We might reverse the charges and just say
It could just have been round about the other way.
Ted Hughes, poet laureate of royal marriages and
    now divorces

once said, that of all public matters he could not but
    notice
that culture, language, identity, who we are, art
are the very pith and permanence and will not depart
the civic stage. So in this Irish-Scottish thing what
    must be taken on board
is who we've been and what we've done, our
    common hoard
of memories, and sharing, beyond statist or sectional
    politics
the divide and conquer band, small fiefdoms, the bag
    of tricks
that screws us up and ties us down and keeps us at a
    loss
for here as there, both us is them and all of them is
    us.

FRENCH LOVE AND BARDS

The initial English invasion ran out of steam in less than a hundred years. Although history books expend many words on describing the English Overlordship between the thirteenth and the sixteenth centuries, it is more because of the availability of their records than of their impact on the life of the overwhelming majority of the people. The English aristocracy lived behind the walls of their fortified manors in Leinster and elsewhere and made some attempts to prevent themselves from being assimilated. Some English was spoken by the descendants of the original invaders in an isolated pocket of south-east Wexford, and by the governing class in Dublin and some other towns. Although English was the language of the administrators in Dublin castle, Irish was the language that assailed their ears as soon as they let down the drawbridge and went about the streets.

The celebrated phrase which describes the settlers as becoming 'more Irish than the Irish themselves' refers to the fact that most of the great 'foreign' families – the Butlers, the Burkes, the FitzGeralds – took on both the colouring and the reality of Irish nobles within a few short generations. Some of them became major patrons of the arts, and in their libraries we find books and manuscripts in Irish, English, French and Latin.

It is likely that it was through the influence of these families that elements of European medieval literature began to find its way into Irish. There was always a strong outside influence on Irish literature since the earliest classical translations of the ninth century. Adapted versions of the *Odyssey* and the *Aeneid* appear in Irish before any other European vernacular, so it is not surprising to find translations of the travels of Maundeville and of Marco Polo, as well as the staple diet of romantic tales finding their way into the language from the fourteenth century on.

More interestingly, however, the tradition of *amour courtois* or courtly love, which seems to have had its beginnings in twelfth-century Provence, had a profound impact on Irish poetry in the first place, and later on, the Irish song tradition. This poetry posits love as a powerful and transforming force, but a force which can be debilitating and destructive where it is frustrated. Although often seen as something entirely new in the history of feeling, it is no more than the local expression of a universal emotion with many similar manifestations in other cultures and times. Greek, Roman and Persian poetry as well as the latest pop lyrics bear testament to the dementing effects of obsessive love. Courtly love, however, presented it in a particularly expressive package which became quite conventional, and this convention was as common in Irish as it was in other European languages:

> I would die for you, my love,
> For your gentle hand, your breasts of snow,
> Your crimson lips, your side like foam,
> For all of these I would lie low.
>
> Your golden hair, your crafted heel,
> Your joyous talk, your sweet, sweet sound,
> Your maiden look, your dreaming eye,
> For all of these I would lie down.

The Irish contribution was somewhat different because it was often composed in the strict metres of the Irish professional poets, or by poets who had received a similar training. The Irish *dánta grá*, or love poems, show that the literary tradition at its strongest could marry the new with the old and provide continuity and innovation without any conflict. A confident culture is always an assimilating one, and the Gaelic culture of the later medieval period not only swallowed up the people who first came to destroy it, but also grafted their expression to its own devices.

The Irish professional poetry which gave shape to these *amour courtois* verses was a very ancient business. There were certainly professional poets functioning in pre-Christian times. They were part of the general druidic caste, the druids being an umbrella term meaning anybody with traditional learning whether legal, religious or literary. With the spread of Christianity the new priests took over the religious functions, the legal profession began to codify their laws in writing, and the poets continued to do what poets do best, posing and composing in equal measure.

When we speak of poets within the Irish context before modern times we are speaking about a particular class of person. They bear little or no resemblance to the notion of the writer as a private whinger, offloading his anguish in brief lyrical gasps before sticking his head in the oven. The Irish word for the traditional poet is *file*, which initially meant a seer or a visionary, but which also contained the strong sense of a learned person. There was a less exalted type of poet known as a *bard* – a mere jingler of jangles – but which word is sometimes used interchangeably with the other. The poet was believed to have supernatural powers and could inflict physical blemishes by the jab of his satire. Although scars and pox and warts were as common amongst the Irish aristocracy at this time as they were amongst every aristocracy at all times, it is not known how much of this was due to the badmouthing of the poets.

They were a powerful hereditary caste, one of the most important of the professional class known collectively as *Aos Dána*. Although this title has recently been re-established to refer to a self-perpetuating oligarchy of state-sponsored writers and artists, its original meaning included blacksmiths, soldiers, magicians, quacks, leeches, househeaters, entertainers and servers of drink. The poet's job was to praise the chief or prince for his bravery and prowess, to decorate these lies in fine words, to flatter, to toady and to kowtow. In return for his services the poet was paid with land, with cattle and with the normal favours which are in the giving of a lord. The chief received a political and cultural service which validated his position and made him feel important. Although poets were generally in the employment of one chief they could move around if they were unhappy with their lot and seek a better position from a rival.

These poets received a training in specially established schools of poetry. This training could take as long as seven years which does not seem excessive when we see the intricate and elaborate metres they were required to master. The stanza of an Irish bardic poem – as this poetry is generally now called – is an intricate intermeshing of carefully patterned syllables. These were governed by strict rules which were part of the syllabus of the schools of poetry. One famous description of these schools refers to poets being given an exercise by their master and then being asked to retire to their beds in the dark 'with a stone upon their bellies' in order to pump their brains for inspiration. The composition was initially oral. This makes perfect sense when we remember that the poem was to be recited or sung at an official occasion before the chief and his retinue. It also helps to remind us that these poems are primarily sound pictures from an aesthetic point of view, whereas their meaning is first and foremost an act of political employment.

Poets often belonged to particular hereditary literary dynasties, like for example the O'Higgins or the O'Daly families. These could often be in charge of the schools also, schools that functioned as places of secular learning from the twelfth century onwards alongside the longer established monasteries. One of the most important results of their work was their regulation and codification of the language. They established a written standard which was accepted all over the Irish-speaking world so that it is now difficult to tell, except by the information on historical events mentioned in the poem itself, when any piece of writing was composed between the twelfth and the seventeenth centuries. This linguistic stability is a sign of the self-confidence of Gaelic culture for nearly 500 years despite whatever machinations were going on against them in the English-dominated Pale.

Although exceptional in many ways, the career of the poet Muiríoch Albanach Ó Dálaigh, anglicised as Scottish Murray O'Daly, is also illustrative of the ways of the poet. He was born into the traditional poetic family of O'Dalys around 1180. Several of his brothers were also poets, so it is not surprising that he got the grounding that he did. He comes to our attention as poet to the O'Connors of Sligo, who were underlings to the more powerful O'Donnell in Donegal. When one of O'Donnell's tax-collectors came to get his dues, Murray reacted as many people would like to do with their persistent taxman. He upped with an axe and smashed his head in. He seemed to be surprised when O'Donnell didn't accept this with equanimity, and was less pleased when he had to flee for his life from O'Donnell's revenge. He wrote a poem which might be summarised as: 'Well, yes, I did murder the guy. But what's the big deal? He was only a lowly servant!' This, in itself, tells us a lot about the arrogance and snobbery of the poetic class which saw itself above the common herd and above the law.

Murray himself spent some fruitless time looking for employment from chieftains in Connacht and Munster, writing them flattering poems and sending them begging letters. He eventually had to escape to Scotland where he became professor of poetry to the Earls of Lennox near present-day Dumbarton. He wrote much conventional verse as he was required to do, but we also find deeply felt personal poetry about his own anguish and loss. One of these is a heartbroken lament on the death of his wife which gives the lie to the rather quaint notion that people in medieval times were incapable of personal expression. He left Dumbarton, probably after the death of his employer, and embarked on a pilgrimage to the Holy Land on the coat tails of the sixth crusade. We know that he returned to Ireland after this in order to effect a reconciliation with O'Donnell. He may have attempted to use the good offices of his friend Cathal Crovderg, King of Connacht, to this end but it seems to have been of no avail. Most probably he returned to Scotland, as many of his poems survived in manuscript there, and it is there also that we find an unbroken line of poets from his time unto the beginning of the nineteenth century who are descended from him.

In the story of this one poet we have the training, the arrogance, the pride, the passion, the travel, the professionalism, the personal, the toadying, the Christianity, the cosmopolitanism, the friendliness with the big and mighty, and the hereditary strain which marked their caste.

Literature also continued to flourish in the monasteries, or under the patronage of learned families. Through medieval times, centres of learning began to put their manuscripts into larger compilations or books. These are usually known by the place in which they were compiled, for example, the Book of Ballymote, the Book of Fermoy, the Book of Glendalough, and the Book of Lismore, although some books are named differently. They are important because in them are preserved the greater part of Irish literature and history of their times – stories, sagas, lives of saints, genealogies, medical texts, translations, lore of places and poetry. These books and manuscripts were the libraries of the Irish before the advent of printing.

CULTURAL PLANNING

Cultures and languages do not wax and wane by the vagaries of the so-called free market. They grow or weaken because of political and economic decisions. Spontaneity is not a feature of cultural change. The introduction of literacy into Ireland strengthened the language and added to its prestige. The Irish Dal Riada chiefs brought Gaelic to Scotland and consolidated its position with a series of military victories. Similarly, the inroads made by English into Ireland were as a result of military and demographic policies in the first instance, and of what would now be called language planning in the second.

In fact, English was not much used at all for administrative purposes for the first couple of hundred years of English involvement in the country. Latin was the main legal language in the thirteenth and fourteenth centuries, being joined by French as time went on. There was some use of English by the Corporation of Waterford from the second half of the fourteenth century onwards, and it had become dominant in the statute book of Galway by the late fifteenth century. By contrast with this, the gaelicised Earls of Kildare, although often steering a middle ground politically, kept their rental books in Latin around 1300, but in the fifteenth and sixteenth centuries they are always in Irish. Both Latin and French remained the chief government official languages throughout the country, and even in Dublin, until the growing English nationalism of Henry VII in the sixteenth century promoted English in all domains of life.

Henry VIII's Act for the English Order, Habit and Language in 1537 was only one of several statutes designed to promote the English language and to curtail the use of Irish and its attendant culture. Designed primarily for 'the King's true subjects' it required that they should 'use and speak commonly the English tongue and language' and should promote 'the English tongue, language, order and condition'. This, on the face of it, appears to be a logical follow-up to the Statutes of Kilkenny enacted nearly 300 years previously, which although written in French, also promoted the English language among the English, and forbade many Irish customs including their hair-do, dress code and manner of riding horses! The general linguistic picture of government officials and of foreign travellers from the fourteenth century to the late sixteenth is one of whatever isolated pockets of the English language that remained being under pressure from Irish.

There is, however, some ambiguity also on the Irish side. It is true that Irish was used in Henry VIII's Dublin Parliament of 1541 because very few of the native Irish chiefs who deigned to attend understood English. But there is also evidence of a growing knowledge of that language among some of them in the following years. We are told that McGillapatrick of Carlow spoke 'good Inglisshe' at that parliament and there are letters from others to Henry in passable English. On the other hand, Latin remained the main language of intercourse between the Irish chiefs and the English administrations, although on other occasions the Irish used their own language as a matter of choice.

It seems likely that speakers of both languages had a good deal of mutual respect for one another. It is true that English commentators of the time liked to contrast their own 'civilitie' with the crude 'barbaritie' of the woodkernes, gallowglasses and lesser breeds without the English Pale. This is just the normal stuff of colonial discourse. There is a famous woodcut by the English traveller John Derricke in his book of engravings, *The Image of Irelande with a Discovery of the Woodkarne* (1581), which shows a sequential picture of an Irish chief tucking into an outdoor feast. His wife, or one of them, sits at his right shoulder wrapped in skins against the Irish weather, while a tonsured monk officiates at his left. The table from which they eat is placed on the earth, while they sit in a hole in the ground which has been especially dug for the day. The beast which is being cooked looks suspiciously like a little child, and a haughty bard chants verses to the accompaniment of a harpist. Most interestingly, two men appear along the side of the picture with their trousers down around their ankles and their bums pointed towards the chief. Although this may seem like they are farting in tune with the poetry, a cartoon-like stream from one of them says 'Look, reader, this is how my parents taught me.'

The implication is clear. The Irish are a crude and impolite people and require to be civilised. The Tudors and the Elizabethans themselves are quite direct about this. They speak of the *conquest* of Ireland and set about it with clear determination.

In the 1560s the English government spent only about £27,000 per annum on Ireland. By 1595 this had risen to £200,000 in one year. At the beginning of Elizabeth I's reign there were only 1200 English fighting men in the country. By the time of the battle of Kinsale in 1601 there were 20,000.

And yet there was ambiguity about the Elizabethan position with regard to the Irish language. Elizabeth herself showed an interest in the language and had a learner's primer made for her by Christopher Nugent, the Baron of Delvin in Co Westmeath. He was a brother of an important Irish poet who was also well-regarded for a time in the English court and whom one author has added to the lists as a contender for the authorship of Shakespeare's plays! This, in its way, shows how the Irish and English aristocracies intermingled and may have been a part of the reason why the Irish language was not held in universal disapproval.

The other reason was religious. Since the time of Henry VIII the Protestant Reformed religion became a vital part of the new English nationalism. There was, therefore, a conflict within expanding and aggressive English nationalism for quite a long time between the suppression of other cultures and the use of their languages for the purposes of spreading the Protestant religion. To force the Irish to stop their tongues with English would delay the opening of their ears to the new faith.

It was for this reason that Elizabeth gave money for the setting up in Ireland of the first printing fount in Irish which resulted in the publication of a catechism and prayer-book for the use of the Church of Ireland in 1571. Although the credit for the first printed book in Irish goes to Seon Carsuel's Calvinist *Foirm na nUrrnuidheadh* in Edinburgh four years previously, Elizabeth's Irish initiative gave a kick-start to publishing in the language in Dublin. These books from the Protestant presses stimulated Catholic response from the Irish colleges on the continent so that the first half of the seventeenth century becomes the richest in our printed book culture until we come to the turn of the twentieth.

Yet a further reason for Elizabethan respect for the Irish language would quite simply be the question of numbers. One contemporary of Shakespeare speaks of his English tongue being of 'small reach'. By this he meant that it hardly extended beyond the bounds of their own kingdom. There were dribbles and rivulets in Wales, and much of southern Scotland spoke a language which would now be classified as English but which then was going its own way. And there were parts of England where the original Celtic speech had not yet been extirpated, particularly in Cornwall and in Cumbria. No Englishman had yet set foot on the New World and the British Empire was a place on which the sun had not yet begun to come up.

At the same time Irish was the language of the entire island of Ireland apart from the English themselves. It was also the language of the greater part of Scotland, and called such by Irish, Scots and English. 'Gaelic' became a much later usage in Scotland, and is hardly ever used to refer to the language in Ireland. Given the lack of any definite population data we can only surmise as to the number of speakers of either language at the beginning of the seventeenth century.

A reasonably common estimate of the population of England is about five million, whereas the Irish-speaking population of the two countries in which it was the main language must have been considerably more than two million. Whatever the actual figures there was no huge difference in absolute terms. English had bigger cities and more books; Irish had a wider geographical spread.

There was no reason to suppose that the fortunes of the two languages and cultures would change so dramatically in the next hundred years.

In 1607 the Irish political leadership went into exile, chopping the intellectual and social head off the country, and, in the same year, English pirate adventurers settled in Jamestown, in what is now the United States.

FRAGMENTATION AND RETREAT

The seventeenth century is the most pivotal century of disaster for Gaelic culture. It did not 'die' after the Battle of Kinsale (1601) but was severely clobbered. The Irish fought three great wars (1593–1601; 1641–53; 1689–91) in the course of the seventeenth century against the English and got hammered in each of them. Although these are often seen in crudely political terms, they were also wars between Irish-speakers or bearers of Gaelic culture and those who were bent on their destruction. Traditional Gaelic society went into exile in September 1607, when the Ulster leaders decided that Spanish wine would give them more hope than Donegal poteen, although they may have been mistaken. The War of the Confederation (1641–53) between an alliance of regal Irish and more progressive off-with-their-heads nationalists against Cromwellian English-only republicans resulted in the deportation of the landed Irish leaders to the badlands of Connacht, and the exile of intellectuals and disaffected as slaves and chattels to the West Indies. Each war was a step down on the ladder for the normal Irish speaker.

Culture is more easily spoken of as something apart from life, those bits that can be plucked and packaged and placed before us. We are not inclined to notice culture when it is the same thing as life.

Until the beginning of the seventeenth century Gaelic and Irish culture were more or less coterminous.

Those who spoke English as their first language were the small numbers of English settlers in Ireland or representatives of English power. The Irish spoke Irish. Some of the Irish nobles had begun to acquire a knowledge of English, but some of the English in the towns could and did speak Irish. There was a bilingual pattern emerging which depended on mutual contact.

Irish was used in all spheres of social and intellectual life. When the nobles wrote to one another, or made contracts, or established treaties, they did so in Irish. When dealing with foreign affairs where they did not use Latin, Irish was likewise used. It was the language of learning whether scientific, medical, philosophical or literary.

It was the language of normality.

But at the end of the seventeenth century whatever was left of the Irish aristocracy mostly spoke English to one another. The Irish in the towns and cities were becoming anglicised. The language was no longer used for learned scientific or discursive purposes, although a rich imaginative literature continued to be composed. It was no longer heard universally in some midland Leinster counties and in much of eastern Ulster.

It was a language in retreat.

This dramatic change prompts the question *Why?*

Early on the morning of 12 July 1691, two armies of about 20,000 men each faced each other across boggy terrain near Ballinasloe, in Co Galway. Although one army was loyal to the deposed King James II and the other to the deposer King William of Orange, and although again history now refers to them as Jacobites and Williamites, and although even more they were made of men of many nationalities who were in their own minds fighting for different causes, there is no doubt that the native Irish saw it as a battle for their own way of life. The fighting did not begin until about 3 o'clock in the afternoon. The better-trained and more powerfully gunned Williamite English forces slowly drove the Irish Jacobites back, despite their fine fortifications. On the other hand, the Irish seemed to be drawing their enemy into a trap where they could be surrounded and slaughtered. Like other battles, this one may have turned on chance. A cannon ball, never the most accurate firepower, blew off the head of the French leader of the Irish army, and his replacement did not have the resolution to retrieve the situation. The day was quickly lost with the result that as many as 7,000 of the Jacobite army were butchered, along with hundreds of their officer corps. Three months later the entire Irish war effort collapsed and their leaders signed the Treaty of Limerick which led the remnants of their army into exile and ushered in the Penal Laws.

This was the last time before the War of Independence (1917–1921) when we could speak of a worthwhile Irish army, under the command of natural military leaders with appropriate training. Its destruction completed the conquest of the country and exposed its society to rampant anglicisation.

That conquest was not the result of one battle. The change of status and strength of Gaelic culture between the beginning of the seventeenth century and its end was the result of three great wars between the English crown and the Irish polity. In each of these wars the Irish lost. The settlement of each war introduced greater English control and the consequent spread of the English language.

Two illustrative examples are enough: After the earlier exile of another generation of Irish political leaders in 1607 the English government decided to settle their lands with people from lowland Scotland and parts of England. Although the plans for this plantation were drawn up in 1609 it was some years before a substantial number of people began to arrive. But they continued to do so throughout the century with the result that there were about 150,000 people of Scottish descent and 20,000 of English descent in concentrated clusters of Ulster within three generations. Most of these were English speakers – although it is certain that a goodly number spoke Gaelic, while many others spoke a dialect of English variously known as Scots or Lallans, which can have a claim to being a separate language.

If we compare the Irish language to a lake, then we might say that the plantation of Ulster and some lesser plantations not often spoken of, introduced a dried-up patch for the first time. The story of the decline of the Irish language is a story of the onward march of those dried-up patches, with the water in the lake becoming more shallow while gaps appear between the pools of retreating dampness. After several centuries the lake itself is largely dried-up with only a few blobs remaining, and the cracks in the floor the only sign remaining that this place once was covered in water.

But the water was also drained off. After the Cromwellian

conquest of 1654 many of the native landowners in Leinster were transplanted to generally poorer land in Connacht, and thousands of prisoners of war, clergy and poorer people were transported to the new British colonies in the West Indies. They brought their language with them. Nothing new to Connacht, but beginning an Irish-speaking colony in some West Indian islands which may have lasted into the nineteenth century.

Despite the fact that the seventeenth century is the great watershed in Gaelic culture, transforming it from a full civil society from top to tail into a peasant culture along the bottom, it is still a century pre-eminent in Irish literature. Part of the great flurry of literary activity was prompted by the realisation that Ireland – as understood by the artistic class – was being destroyed. Séathrún Céitinn's (Geoffrey Keating) *Foras Feasa ar Éirinn* and *The Annals of the Kingdom of Ireland* were both completed in the 1630s. The first is a massive history of Ireland written from the native viewpoint; the second is a vast compilation of records of historical material which is invaluable for our understanding of the period before the seventeenth century. Keating's was written largely in reply to racist distortions of Irish history, while the annals were a response to the wholesale destruction of Irish manuscript material.

The great poetic theme of the century is the loss of patronage and prestige by the poets themselves. If this appears a selfish preoccupation then it is. On the other hand, it does mirror what was happening. The poets fully realised, long before Marx, that artistic and imaginative culture survives and breathes and has its being in material stuff like money and land and the leisure they bring. Remove the material base and all your fancies disappear. They saw this as clear as the writing on the wall or the mist upon the bog.

A truly magnificent poet such as Dáibhí Ó Bruadair

(1624–1698) began his career with training in a traditional bardic school and wrote in strict professional metres for rich patrons who supported him. At the end of his life he grovelled around the fag ends of a vanishing Gaelic aristocracy, begging for work or eking out his existence with a spade while he wrote poems of savage indignation in looser unprofessional form. Much of his great poetry is a long meditation and commentary on the state of the country, but it is his shorter works which show the anger and despair of a proud temperament emotionally wounded.

> Pity I'm not a real lout,
> bad enough to be a boor
> so that I could go about
> amongst the fools and poor.

A poem for the children of one of the hereditary poetic families exposes the bitterness:

> After the death of the poets whose wealth was knowledge and verse
> Our fate is despair and mockery and ignorance and what is worse,
> Our books are rotting in corners and their meanings dispersed
> And for their wisdom and beauty our sons do not give a curse.

There was much truth in his complaint. But the destruction of any privileged caste allows for the resurrection of those beneath. From then on the voice of Gaelic Ireland began to sing and to speak from below.

A BOTTOM-UP CULTURE

The eighteenth century brings a culture which reversed the natural order of things. Gaelic society becomes a beheaded society. Whatever lords and ladies gay exist are English or Anglo-Irish implants. The pattern of macular bilingualism which already existed in the towns begins to spread throughout the countryside, with the larger English-speaking spots appearing along the east coast and in the good rich lands where fat cattle could be raised. The colonial big house, the prize of conquest, sat as an island in the middle of a sea of peasants who muttered what broken English they could to their masters while their souls sang in their native tongue underneath their doffing caps.

It is only much later in the century that the 'outside' world began to appreciate what this culture entailed. The wealth of song and of poetry and of story was 'invisible' except to those for whom it was their only cultural expression. And where it was encountered it was not always seen as a thing of beauty, even for those who were otherwise enlightened.

Jonathan Swift, for example, once wrote that he hoped that the Irish language could be quickly extirpated from the kingdom and that it could be done at very little expense. This appears to be a crude statement from someone whose writings are marked by an impassioned humanity. On the other hand it is possible that he was writing with the black irony for which he was so famous. We do not take seriously his modest proposal that Irish children should be sold to be eaten in order to make money for their parents and in order to relieve them of their burden, although there must have been some who did not see the tongue firmly stuck in his cheek. The comment in relation to the Irish language is even more surprising in the case of Swift who was almost certainly acquainted with a circle of Irish writers and scholars who lived in Dublin during his time, and one of whom may have given him the germ of his idea for *Gulliver's Travels* from a native Irish tale.

Swift was also acquainted with his contemporary Turlough Carolan (1670–1738) who is best known as a harper and composer, but who also was an accomplished poet. Carolan's career is emblematic of what was happening to Gaelic culture in the early eighteenth century. On the one hand he is seen as the last of the Irish traditional 'bards' who made his living on the patronage of the aristocracy, even though most of this aristocracy were now the new English colonial landlords. On the other, he mixed with both his own Gaelic poets and the new kind of Anglo-Irish writer such as Swift. He was at home in the city, or the big house, or the countryside. He composed poetry and music out of the native tradition but was also influenced by the Italian composers Corelli and Vivaldi. His compositions which included words and music enabled him to make a good living, and a volume of his music was published in Dublin during his lifetime. This volume is interesting in so far as the music is given prominence and the words are left behind, a distinction which Carolan himself would not have well understood. It was a sign of what was happening to Gaelic culture, however. The accessible bits were being retained for the easy gratification of the ear, while the melodious words were being dumped in the sin-bin of history. Swift did do a version of one of his Irish poems – now known to us as 'O'Rourke's Feast' – but we know Carolan far better through the revival of his music by groups such as The Chieftains.

Other acquaintances of Swift's out of the underbelly of Gaelic Ireland did not fare so well in posterity's stakes. Down the road and around the corner from him lived the poet and scribe Seán Ó Neachtain who was at the centre of a school of Irish writers who worked in the capital. Many of these were from outside Dublin but some, like

Seán himself, were natives of the city. His father Tadhg was a more notable writer and composed one of the few prose works in eighteenth-century Irish which could nearly be described as a novel. But cosmopolitan prose was a difficult child to nurture among a poor urban population who were illiterate in their own language, and must have been mostly unlettered in English also.

The pressure on those people who aspired to rise in the world to become anglicised must have been immense even at this time. The controversial religious philosopher John Toland (1670–1722), for example, although a native speaker of Irish, turned to English and Presbyterianism for his education and career. English was the only way up for someone like him. The dramatist Hugh Kelly (1739–1777) whose plays were a big hit in his lifetime never considered writing in his native Irish. There would have been no future in an Irish-speaking theatre. It seems probable that Edmund Burke (1729–1797) spoke Irish, but that language never claimed his attention as a vehicle for serious intellectual debate.

This all points to a situation which might be summarised in the following diagrams:

Dates by which these social classes had become significantly anglicised

Native aristocracy	c.1650
Professions	c.1700
Urban middle class	c.1720–40
Urban working class	c.1780
Strong farmers	c.1800
Rural poor (east & midlands)	c.1820–40
Rural poor (south & west)	c.1845–90

Dates by which writing in these areas had become significantly anglicised

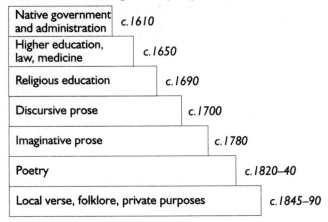

Native government and administration	c. 1610
Higher education, law, medicine	c. 1650
Religious education	c. 1690
Discursive prose	c. 1700
Imaginative prose	c. 1780
Poetry	c. 1820–40
Local verse, folklore, private purposes	c. 1845–90

Despite being attacked from the top and eroded from the east, Gaelic culture in the eighteenth century was vivid and vigorous for those who lived it. The great folk culture of music, song and dance which really only became exposed in the following century throbbed and thrummed away without much comment.

Politics was Jacobite, even for some years after the destruction of their cause in the wake of the Battle of Culloden in 1746. This was because there was always some hope that yet another rotten Stuart would return, and because the Irish could not have known that their white-headed boy had retreated into a bottle. The Irish supported the Stuarts, because the Stuarts were Scots, and the Scots were Irish and we were all one big happy family. Besides, regal politics was the only one that most people knew until the progressives in the French Revolution began shortening the titled spongers by a head. Gaelic Ireland latched on to whatever political ideology was appropriate, just as nationalists became communists and communists became nationalists as the tide turned in our own time. Thus, a fine poet like Mícheál Óg Ó Longáin (1766–1837) could begin his career writing Jacobite poetry, later turn to verse supporting agrarian Whiteboy-type activities, fashion some rousing republican songs at the time of the rebellion of 1798, and end up penning decent sectarian diatribes in the fashion of the time.

Not all literature was just fashion, however. One of the finest Irish poems of the eighteenth century, *Caoineadh Airt Uí Laoghaire* ('The Lament for Art O'Leary'), was composed according to the custom of weeping or 'keening' in a formalised way over a dead person. The former professor of poetry at the University of Oxford, Peter Levi, has described it as 'the greatest poem written in these islands in the whole eighteenth century. I believe that Goethe, and Thomas Gray, and Wordsworth, and Matthew Arnold ... might all have thought so.' Yet when we read it, it appears a strange composition unlike what we normally expect poetry to be. It beats and pulsates with a passion wrought from the most grievous grief and is borne along by anger and despair. Although a literary composition originally, it uses the tradition of lamenting the dead to give it extra power and demented resonance.

Part of its attraction may well have been the romantic story behind it. Eibhlín Dubh Ní Chonaill (Eileen O'Connell) was a young widow when she fell in love with Art O'Leary, an Irish officer in the Austrian army. Both came from families who had managed to retain some wealth in the great dispossessions of the eighteenth century. She was a spirited woman; he was a boastful soldier and a bit of a lad. It was common for the sons of the more important Irish families to serve in Catholic continental armies. She tells us how she fell in love with this fine thing when she spotted him strutting his wares on his white horse. This love at first sight led to marriage, along with the disapproval of her family who were the great O'Connell smugglers of Kerry. Art O'Leary was a trouble-maker and in dispute with the law. After a row over a horse he confronted his adversaries but was shot down and killed. Tradition tells us that his wife rushed to the spot, wept over his body, drank up his blood and composed her great lament. The truth is probably more prosaic, but the legend is better.

> My love forever!
> I never thought they'd get you
> Until your mare came to me
> Her reins trailing groundwards
> Your heart's blood on her shanks
> And smeared across your saddle
> Where you would sit and stand.
> I jumped across the doorway
> I jumped across the gate
> My third jump on your horse.
> I beat my hands with terror
> And galloped across the country
> As fast as my soul could bear
> Until I found your body
> By a stunted bush of furze
> With neither Pope nor bishop
> Nor priest nor any cleric
> To say for you the psalms
> But only a withered beaten woman
> Who shielded you with her cloak
> While your blood gushed from your wounds.
> I didn't wait to clean it
> But lapped it with my tongue.

If this poem seems to come out of the darkness of some primitive rite, *Cúirt an Mheán Oíche* (The Midnight Court) appears to be a work of the Enlightenment. This is particularly so because twentieth-century Ireland is often painted, with some justification, as a place of sexual repression and puritan killjoydom, and this long poem of more than 1000 lines celebrates life and love and lust with uninhibited abandon. It was written by Brian Merriman (1745–1805), about whom little is known. Some commentators choose to see his poem as a commentary on his own illegitimate status with its apparent celebration of free love and excoriation of marital bondage. But this is to reduce it to autobiography and it is too rich a work to allow for any easy interpretation.

The court mentioned in the title of the poem is where the men of Ireland are arraigned before a female judge and jury for their neglect of women in matters of sex, marriage and procreation. It is written in the form of an aisling or vision poem which was a common eighteenth-century device to allow a message of hope and political salvation to be brought to the author by a beautiful young woman from the fairy world. Merriman turns this formula on its head, however, for in place of the beautiful young woman of the convention he is met by a shrieking and terrifying harridan of gigantic proportions who drags him through the muck of the countryside to a kangaroo court at midnight. He there sees a series of confrontations between shirt-scared men and frighteningly articulate women who praise their own sexual exploits, the joys of bastardy and the prowess of priests. The men haven't a chance. Their sentence is not penile servitude but rather a severe flogging with whips and violence and we are not given to understand that any of them were into sado-masochism.

Because of its rollicking humour, its bawdy passages, its pseudo-liberation philosophy and its dramatic structure it has been translated in full at least ten times into English, and several times into other languages. The Irish is superb, using colloquial and literary language to forge a masterpiece in faultless couplets. Despite his strange theories about the poem – he believed it had to be influenced by Robbie Burns even though Burns comes after Merriman, and that such a frankly lusty poem could not come out of Gaelic Ireland – Frank O'Connor's English translation is still the best.

One aspect of the poem puzzled many critics who see a direct linear connection between literature and life. It is the contention put forward by one of the women accusers in the poem that the population of Ireland is falling because the men are neglecting their duties of marriage and seedspreading. The reason for the bemusement is that at no comparable period in Irish history was the population growing so quickly as that from the last decades of the eighteenth century into the great famines of the 1840s. While it is difficult to assess accurately the population in 1780 when Merriman wrote his poem, a figure of around 2,000,000 would not be too far out. When we compare this to the generally accepted figure of about 8,500,000 for 1845 we get some idea of the extent of the population explosion. While Merriman was perfectly aware of this it does not appear anywhere in his poem because, like all great literature, it is a work of the imagination and of the human spirit in the first and in the last instance and not a quarry for social scientists or demographers. It should be read as such.

The population figures hide something else, however. They do not tell us how many people at any time before the famine were Irish or English or bilingual speakers. It is certain that the figures given in the first census in which a language question was asked are woefully inaccurate. This census of 1851 was unfortunate in taking place in the immediate aftermath of the Great Famine. It returned a population of about 6,500,000 of whom about one quarter were Irish speakers. We know it to be crazy in much detail because one of the strongest Irish-speaking areas of the present day in north-west Donegal returned an Irish-speaking population of only between 25–50 per cent

150 years ago. We are led to believe that the language had been abandoned by more than half the population just after the famine but that they returned to it over the next few generations. This would fly in the face of the evidence for language shift in rural communities.

The most obvious explanation is, of course, that Irish was seen as the language of shame and defeat and poverty, and indeed of hunger and failure and death, and should not be admitted to except under duress. The irony is that with the huge increase in population from 1770 to 1845 there was a corresponding increase in the absolute number of Irish speakers. It seems likely that of the population of nearly nine million at the start of the famine, about half were speakers of Irish. There had never been as many Irish speakers before or since as there were in 1845. Irish was not a small or minority or insignificant language in European terms in the middle of the nineteenth century. It had more speakers than Danish, or Norwegian, or Finnish, or Flemish, or Welsh.

There were two major differences, however, between the situation of Irish and that of other languages.

The first is that the famine killed off a lot of them, and many more emigrated. The population of Ireland dropped in about ten years by two-and-a-half million through starvation, disease and emigration, and most of these were speakers of Irish. For the first time in Irish history the language was a minority language in its own country.

The second is that it was now almost entirely the language of only the rural very poor, and was not supported by any legal, administrative, commercial, educational or ecclessiastical institution whatsoever. George Moore remarked that it seemed to him to be 'a language suitable for the celebration of an antique Celtic rite, but too remote for modern use. It had never been spoken by ladies in silken gowns with fans in their hands.'

Whatever about the truth of that, from now on it only had its own intrinsic worth and poetry and music and folklore, and these are no bulwark against the world.

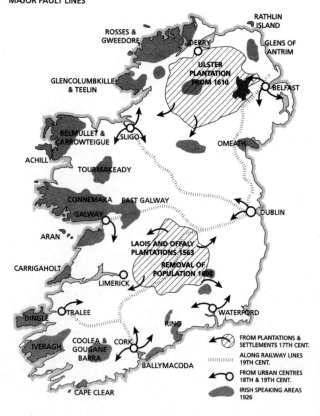

GEOGRAPHICAL EROSION
OF THE IRISH LANGUAGE
1600–1900, INCLUDING
MAJOR FAULT LINES

RATHLIN ISLAND

ROSSES & GWEEDORE

DERRY

GLENS OF ANTRIM

ULSTER PLANTATION FROM 1610

GLENCOLUMBKILLE & TEELIN

BELFAST

BELMULLET & CARROWTEIGUE

SLIGO

OMEATH

ACHILL

TOURMAKEADY

CONNEMARA

EAST GALWAY

GALWAY

DUBLIN

ARAN

LAOIS AND OFFALY PLANTATIONS 1563

CARRIGAHOLT

REMOVAL OF POPULATION 1608

LIMERICK

DINGLE

TRALEE

WATERFORD

RING

IVERAGH

COOLEA & GOUGANE BARRA

CORK

BALLYMACODA

CAPE CLEAR

FROM PLANTATIONS & SETTLEMENTS 17TH CENT.

ALONG RAILWAY LINES 19TH CENT.

FROM URBAN CENTRES 18TH & 19TH CENT.

IRISH SPEAKING AREAS 1926

CLERICS AND POLITICIANS

A culture can often afford to lose its aristocracy but can hardly survive losing its local leaders. The Gaelic aristocracy began leaking away in the first half of the seventeenth century. The scholar Conall Mac Geoghegan, who translated *The Annals of Clonmacnoise* into English as early as 1627, complained that the Irish lords were sending their children to learn English. Máire Rua Mac Mahon (1615–1686), who was born in Bunratty Castle and lived in an equally grand one, came from a family who conducted all their legal business through Irish with the professional lawyers of Clare and Thomond. Her first marriage was to an Irish lord and was an entirely Gaelic affair. Her second was to another Irish lord but the inscription above their castle was carved out in English. Her third marriage was to a Cromwellian officer and she raised her children as Protestants, while her son and heir Donnchadh turned into a Denis overnight.

This is not an unusual occurrence when we consider that the leaders of English society spoke French for 300 years, and that in the eighteenth and nineteenth centuries the Russian aristocracy aped Gallic ways. It was ever the habit of the rich to follow the fashion of the richer.

The loss of local leaders to a culture is a much more serious affair as these are often the mediators between what goes on in an area and the wider social and political powers. The Catholic clergy were the natural leaders of the Irish after the destruction of Gaelic civil society in 1691. While the penal laws were not as severe in practice as they were in intent they did mean the more or less total disaffection of the native clergy from the Protestant state. Many received their education in Catholic countries and in colleges which had fostered Gaelic literacy and learning since the early seventeenth century.

This position did not change until after the destruction of the Stuart cause and the Papal refusal in 1766 to recognise the validity of the Jacobite claim to the English – by this time the British – throne. This made the German royal family in London feel more secure, and they even became more chuffed when the Catholic Church allowed prayers for themselves, their household and government to be said publicly in their places of worship. Close observers of the royal family might have noticed the inefficacy of those prayers given the incidences of insanity and stupidity which were rampant down the Hanoverian lines, but this kind of critical analysis is unusual in royal watchers.

Gradually Catholicism began to rise from its metaphorical knees while remaining firmly planted on its physical ones. But Gaelic culture and Irish language did not rise with it. Although the population placed their bets on Catholicism for the next life, they were taking no chances on material success in this one. The priests used the language as they had to as a means of communication in ordinary life. Irish was the language of confession, Latin of the Mass, and English of education.

There were exceptions, of course. John Carpenter, who was both a native of Dublin's inner city and a native Irish speaker, was Archbishop of Dublin from 1770 to 1786. He published a prayer book in Irish for use in his diocese which was reprinted until 1847. This leads us to believe that there was some native Irish-speaking population in the city until that time. Bishop James Gallagher who died in the mid-eighteenth century published a book of sermons in Irish which went through 23 editions in the following 150 years. This demand and necessity for Irish material did not urge the hierarchy to use the language for their own educational purposes when they were allowed open their own seminaries in the years just before the Act of Union. The Royal College of St Patrick at Maynooth, although based on French models of clerical training, was entirely anglicised in language and political outlook when it was established by act of parliament in 1795. The bishops preferred quiet English domination to 'the rule of French impiety and irreligion' as one of them put it. Even the chair of Irish came from a private benefactor.

The ordinary Irish person was being sucked into the state system, and might even be said to have a stake in it. When Irish Catholics were allowed join the British Army in 1793 in order to provide body fodder for the expanding empire, it represented a further step in the normalisation of relations between the government and the ruled; normalisation here meaning the tendency to accept fully the nature of the British state and to acquiesce in it. Even before this, local Whiteboy movements in the 1760s used English in order to air their grievances and to deal with landlords, factors and magistrates. Their leaders called themselves Captain Firebrand, or Captain Billhook, or Captain Dreadnought. English was from that time seen as the language of politics, even for the common people.

It was no surprise, then, that the great political orator, agitator, barrister, parliamentarian, Catholic rentcollector and emancipator, Daniel O'Connell (1775–1847), although a native speaker of Irish, used only English in his public affairs. This was in keeping with his own utilitarian beliefs and with those of his followers. Even when addressing mass rallies of tens of thousands of people in the west of Ireland, he spoke to them in English – a language they did not understand. There is some irony in his speaking to a meeting in Clifden in English when nobody understood him, and de Valera speaking to a similar meeting in the same place 100 years later in Irish and nobody understanding him. This reflects not only the language change, but also the understanding of language as symbol by two great political leaders. For the pre-famine Irish, English was *the* symbol of political discourse.

This is also evident from the use of newspapers and

ballads. As O'Connell began to politicise the countryside his movement for the repeal of the Act of Union produced cheap newspapers which were available in reading rooms in the towns. They were also read aloud in the houses of the ordinary people and translated into Irish when necessary. The magic of reading to an illiterate population cannot be overestimated, and when this magic is linked to another language it becomes even more powerful. It became quite irresistible with the foundation of the *Nation* newspaper in 1842, which despite the favourable attitude of some of its founders towards Irish, was written entirely in English. It is claimed that at its height it had more than a quarter of a million readers, but we may be confident that it had even more hearers, through domestic and local channels of telling and translating.

Ballads in English became a half-way house between traditional Irish and bourgeois concert-hall songs. Although there are hundreds of Gaelic political songs, many of them are Jacobite or deal with O'Connell or Parnell as if they were yet another Louis or Stuart coming to save them. The ballad tradition in English is far more political than the Irish song tradition from 1798 onwards. 'The Boys of Wexford,' 'The Shan Van Vocht', 'The Wearing of the Green', 'Bold Robert Emmet' and hundreds of others became immensely popular through the activities of broadsheet peddlars who sold their wares at fairs and gatherings.

The single most important form of literary publishing for the ordinary person in the nineteenth century was the production of ballads either in book or in broadsheet form. They were the kind of songs that would have been composed in Irish if the language was not being abandoned by its own people, and if it was seen as the language of the new politics and patriotism – which it was not. It was another sign that Gaelic Ireland was becoming, on the one hand, an unreadable world, but on the other was beginning to transform itself into something new.

OLD BOOKS AND NEW COVERS

After the great famines even the rural poor began to ditch the language with great abandon. Some of this was the sheer necessity of knowing English in order to gain an advantage in America, where millions of them were going. A great deal of the language shift came from straight-forward colonised cultural cringe and from the redneck shame of being forever nobodies. There were cases of parents who knew no English refusing to speak to their children for fear they would pick up the dreaded Irish tongue, with the result that a great silence fell over the land. English flowed to the people from pulpit and press, from the mouths of politicians and proselytisers, it spread out from the towns which had been originally garrisoned by British soldiers and police, it was diffused by centres of trade and commerce, it sped down the railway lines and followed the coaches, it crawled out towards remote hamlets and up the sides of the hills, it obliterated songs and stories and sagas and prayers and practices and placenames. It changed Ireland forever.

This change had been well observed for several generations previous to this and was sometimes regretted. The more culturally aware responded in two ways. The first may be called the antiquarian and the second the transformative, and in their own ways they both helped to encourage the cultural revival which commenced at the end of the nineteenth century.

The attempt to retrieve, or at least to recover, the past may have originally taken place with music. Without the work of the great collectors of Irish music many thousands of Irish airs, tunes and melodies would now be irretrievably lost. The revival of Irish music is often dated from the Belfast Harp Festival of 1792, although there were similar festivals in Granard ten years previously. The Harp Festival was not sponsored by the United Irishmen, but it was part of the same cultural ferment of Belfast that threw up an interest in the rights of man and in political brotherhood. It was no accident that it took place on the third anniversary of the storming of the Bastille. In Ireland, politics and culture always maintained a symbiotic relationship.

Ten harpers turned up, six of them blind, all of them old, and one almost 100 years of age. A young man called Edward Bunting was employed to write down the music as they played. We still have his notebook, and it is the oldest manuscript of Irish music that we possess. But Bunting also went into the field, travelling extensively in Munster and Connacht. He brought with him a schoolmaster from County Down called Patrick Lynch whose job it was to note down the Irish words which acccompanied the music. The realisation by Bunting and his employers that the words and the music were part of the same art was vital in the further study and promotion of Irish music. They were pioneers who were followed by the likes of George Petrie (1789–1866), William Forde (1759–1850), John Edward Pigot (1822–1871), James Goodman (1828–1896) and some others whose total collection amounts to something like 10,000 airs in about a century of work. Throughout the nineteenth century Irish music was treated with the same disdain and snootiness as was the language. It was despised by respectability and laughed at by the music hall. Yet, it blossomed in the twentieth century and became known as one of the great folk music cultures of the world. It is one of the great success stories of Gaelic culture.

The same urge to preserve and to study was the impetus behind many learned societies and Irish language classes. As the language waned the societies and the primers waxed. Classes in the language were being taught in the Belfast Academy in 1795 and were promoted 'by the advantages it affords to the students of Irish and Eastern Antiquities, especially to those who wish to acquire the knowledge of Druidical Theology and worship as sketched by Caesar and Tacitus'. Dr Johnson had previously recommended the study of Irish 'to those who are curious either in the original of nations or the affinities of languages, to be further informed of the revolutions of a people so ancient and once so illustrious'.

The implication is clear. A study of Irish would not only unlock some of the mysteries of history, but would cast light into the beginnings of speech and religion. The Scottish poet Alasdair Mac Mhaighistir Alasdair had written a eulogy for the Gaelic or Irish tongue in 1738, in which he said:

> Si labhair Adhamh
> Ann à pharras fèin
> 'S ba shiublach Gàidhlig
> O bheul àlainn Eubh.

> It was what Adam spoke
> In his garden of Paradise
> And Gaelic flowed freely
> From Eve's beautiful mouth.

Although composed with tongue in cheek it does reflect the debates about the original language of the world which had been going on since medieval times. Philology was a crude and rough tool in the early nineteenth century and little enough was known about the relationship between languages. The early Celtic scholar Edward Lhuyd (1660–1709) had posited some affinity between Irish and Welsh, but it wasn't until the work of European scholars and in particular the publication of Johann Kaspar Zeuss's *Grammatica Celtica* in 1853 that the position of Irish in the family tree of languages was firmly established.

Irish is a Celtic language. This simply means that it is related to other languages which we also call Celtic. These languages are, in turn, part of a larger extended family known as the Indo-European languages. The theory is that there was an Indo-European tribe or nation some thousands of years ago who spread across Europe and India and whose tongues forked into Germanic and Slavonic and Latin and Celtic and Indo-Iranian speech. These, in turn, as the forests closed in on them and as they moved from their mother berth, in the case of Germanic, split into German, Danish, Dutch, English, Swedish, Faroese and Icelandic. This means that Irish is a distant relation of Sanskrit and Hindustani and Persian and Bengali. One example of this connection is that the great Genghis *Khan* carries in his name the same word as the Irish *ceann*, which simply means 'head', exactly what he was. (See diagram on page 87.)

The Celts likewise kept splitting apart. First there were the Continental Celts on mainland Europe and the Insular Celts in Ireland and Britain. Then by some twist of the mouth the Insular Celts split into what linguists call 'p' Celts and 'q' Celts, which meant that some of them didn't pronounce their 'p's while the others couldn't manage their 'q's. The Britons, in general, were of the 'p' variety; the Irish of the 'q'. When St Patrick came to Ireland the natives were unable to say his name, Patricius, and pronounced it *Quotricius*, which became *Cothraige* in Old Irish.

Modern Irish is, therefore, a cousin of Welsh and Breton, but a sibling of Scottish Gaelic and Manx. A good Irish speaker will understand some Scottish Gaelic, but they are by no means mutually intelligible. They shared a common culture and identity until the conquest of Scotland after 1746. Manx would be better understood by the Irish if it were alive. Revived or learned Manx is grammatically easier than Irish, but it suffers from a barbaric orthography based on English which was imposed on the language in

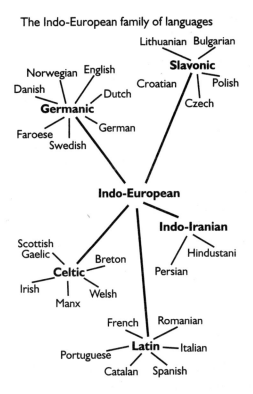

The Indo-European family of languages

the early seventeenth century.

The scholarly interest in Irish led to the foundation of several important learned societies such as the Gaelic Society of Dublin (1806), the Iberno-Celtic Society (1818), and the Irish Archaeological Society (1840). The Ulster Gaelic Society (1830) was interested in more than learning just for itself. They sought also to publish useful books in Irish for reading purposes, and did in fact publish translations of two of Maria Edgeworth's stories. Although the Royal Irish Academy was in the business of antiquarianism since 1785, it increased its involvement in Irish studies during the nineteenth century, particularly with the employment of such a powerful scholar genius as Eugene O'Curry (1794–1862) who worked with another indefatigable scholar John O'Donovan (1806–1861) on the Ordnance Survey of Ireland.

The work of the survey was both scholarly and practical. O'Donovan traipsed the country finding the correct Irish word for parish and place, townland and topography. Brian Friel's play *Translations* maps the change in his small town of Ballybeg from Irish names to English names, and the cultural destruction that ensued. The vast majority of names of Irish towns and countryside are anglicisations or translations or misunderstandings or corruptions of the Irish.

On the road from Dublin to the south, drivers will spot a sign which says *Kill*. This is not an invitation to murder anybody but a phonetic rendering of the Irish word *cill* in a placename which means a church. The name is very common, as in Killarney, Kilkeel, Killaloo, Kilbeggan, Kilmurray, Kilkenny, Kildare, Kilcock. *Bally* is probably the most common element in Irish placenames: Ballylongford, Ballycotton, Ballyhooley, Ballymena, Ballyshannon, Ballina, Ballymahon, Ballybofey, Ballyjamesduff, Ballydehob. It derives from the Irish *baile*, meaning a settlement or a cluster of houses, although occasionally the 'bally' can mean 'the mouth of a ford'. *Dún*, a defence or fortress, gives us Dundalk, Dungarvan, Dunmanway, Dunshaughlin, Downpatrick, Dunkettle, Dungannon, Dunleer, Donegal. *Ros*, a wood or a headland, is found in Roscommon, Rossanowlagh, Roscarbery, Roscrea, Rosslare, New Ross, Rosapenna, although we must needs be sometimes careful as Rostrevor is from Rose Trevor, the third wife of a landlord who named his estates and properties after her in his uxoriousness. *Cluain*, a meadow or grazing field, is in Clonmel, Clontarf, Clones, Clonbur, Clonmany. *Carraig*, a rock, pops up in Carrick-on Suir, Carrick-on-Shannon,

Carrickfergus, Carrickmacross, and in innumerable Carricks. We find *Inis* on the names of islands, Inishvickillaune, Inishbofin, Inishmurray, Inishtraholl since it is one of the Irish words for an island.

To understand the Irish language is to be able to read the landscape. Every townland and field and promontory means something. Folklorists discovered in *Gaeltachtaí* or Irish-speaking districts, that some people had names for rocks and nooks and hillocks and rivulets. The land was alive with the sound of names, and their meaning had not yet been garbled.

To the untrained eye many names appear strange and exotic. They all cover some kind of story or shape. How about: Cargaghlisnanarney, the rocky land of the fairy fort of the berries; Legmuckduff, the hollow ground of the black pig; Mohernameela, the thicket of the hornless cow; Cappaghvuckle, the tillage plot of the drove of swine; or Tobernamoodane, the well of the stumps left on a furze hill after the scythe or hook?

A similar process took place with the anglicisation of names. The practice of taking surnames only commenced for the common people some time in the seventeenth century, although the habit had probably been introduced with the Anglo-Norman invasion. They initially became important among leading families who owned large chunks of land. The Irish way of naming was simply to call somebody after one of their parents like, for example, Mícheál Phádraig (i.e. Patrick's Michael), or including a grandparent, Sorcha Bhid Sheáin (John's Brigid's Sarah). This form of naming is still the usual colloquial practice in *Gaeltachtaí*.

Irish surnames are generally recognised in their Gaelic form by the use of *Mac* and *Ó*. Originally meaning 'son of' and 'grandson' or 'descendant of' respectively, they have been anglicised as 'Mc', 'Mac' and 'O'. Thus, *Mac Cárthaigh* becomes 'McCarthy' in English, and *Ó Mathúna* becomes

O'Mahoney. Many other names simply lost their Irish-signifying *Mac* or *Ó*, as in *Mac Consaidín* transmuting into 'Considine', or *Ó Fearghail* being reduced to 'Farrell'. These names became turned into English forms by the actions of English administrative officials who couldn't get their tongues around the strange sounds which assailed their ears and who then made a stab at something which approximated the original.

As a result of this haphazard policy many famous Irish names took on multiple Englishings. *Mac Dómhnaill*, for example, can turn up as McDonnell, MacDonnell, MacDonald, Daniels, McDaniels, Donald, Donaldson, without pushing the permutations too far. The Irish *Ó hAodha* or *Mac Aoidh* can give us Hayes, McHugh, Magee, McKee, Keyes, Hughes, McCoy, McKay, MacKew, Hewson, Huston and variations thereon. Other names took on an English form that was similar in appearance to the Irish. Thus, *Ó Cuinneagáin* becomes 'Cunningham', or *Mac an Iomaire* can be made into a fancy 'Montgomery'.

A similar fate overtook personal names, although these are much more susceptible to fashion than those of families. You have no choice about your surname, but you can pick any first name you like. There was a wealth of native Irish names that began to fall into disuse under Anglo-Norman influence. During the medieval period the common stock of Jewish New Testament names took hold, and are probably still the most frequently used. But as the Irish cultural revival grew in strength from the 1880s onwards it became fashionable again to give children native Gaelic names. It might be said that one of the more obvious successes of the cultural revival through the twentieth century is the enduring practice of giving children Irish names. Therefore names such as Fionnuala, Ciara, Caoimhe, Aoife, Bróna, Éadaoin, Aisling and Eithne are quite popular with girls, something that would have been inconceivable 150 years ago.

This change in favour of a native turn began in the early years of the nineteenth century with the renewed interest in Gaelic culture among the learned. This was a turn that was initially antiquarian but eventually changed to a living force. This change did not come with the political programme of Daniel O'Connell who, in his heyday (1824–41), spoke English only to his massed rallies throughout Irish-speaking Munster and Connacht. The implications were clear. English was the language of progress and of politics and therefore of the future. Irish and Gaelic meant 'culture'; English meant life and the music of what makes things happen. If his listeners hadn't the least clue about what he said they certainly knew it was wise and was attached to power and to influence. English was magic and opened ears; Irish was homely and didn't reach beyond the next town.

There were close on nine million people in Ireland at the outbreak of the Great Famine in 1845. About half of them were speakers of Irish as their first tongue, more than there had ever been before at any one time in Irish or Scottish history. Most of them were poor. The poor died and the slightly less poor emigrated. The Irish speakers perished and where they had enough to hang on in there they also emigrated. Irish was the language of most of the people of the country in 1830; by 1860 it was the language of a minority for the first time in three or four or five thousand years. This was a change beyond measure. It was France without French, it was England without Shelley, Keats and Dickens. Even Gaelic culture itself in its fastnesses beyond the reach of respectabilising bourgeoisification became impoverished. In nineteenth-century Irish literature, it is often hard to tell the good from the lees, and much low-falutin' stuff is elevated to the status of art. The great sagas become shredded and garbled and the great stories of Ireland are normality is reduced to the slurry furred-tongue patois of forelock-tugging, knuckle-dragging peasantry. Very few people could comprehend that the new Irish comical dimwit-friendly version of English would grow to great artistic promise within two generations.

The literary class initially took a different view, however. As Irish began to recede from the east before the famine and flee in full retreat into the west afterwards, many writers in English attempted to capture the spirit of what they imagined was going for ever. Jeremiah J. Callanan (1795–1829), for example, made serious attempts to turn Irish poetry and song into English, and was one of the first to learn the language and collect folklore for that purpose. Francis Sylvester Mahony (1804–1866) who wrote under the pseudonym of Fr Prout echoed the rhythms and structure of the older language to support his own. Even Thomas Moore (1779–1852) in his famous *Melodies* successfully filched Bunting's airs for his own graceful songs, as part of a general project to make Irish culture open to the English. While William Hazlitt accused Moore of converting 'the wild harp of Erin into a musical snuff-box', he does stand at the beginning of a long line of writers who tried to wrestle with the matter of Ireland in the shadow of the Irish language.

CULTURAL REVIVAL

Something changed in Irish cultural life towards the end of the nineteenth century. We may put the date at 1884 with the foundation of the Gaelic Athletic Association (GAA), or the publication of the first volume of poetry of WB Yeats in 1886, or Douglas Hyde's bilingual collection of folklore *Beside the Fire* in 1890, or the death of Parnell in 1891, or the beginning of the Gaelic League in 1893, but they were all part of the same ferment. Some time during those years a slumbering beast awoke, putting on new skins and struggling towards the new century to be born.

There is a play by Críostóir Ó Floinn entitled *Mise Raifteirí* ('I am Raftery') based on the life and influence of the poet Antoine Raiftearaí (1779–1835). The play makes the pitch that while the life was interesting, the influence was more pervasive still. If the play can be said to have an argument it might be put like this: Raiftearaí lived among his people and made songs that became immensely popular; these songs were remembered by the public; Lady Gregory became fascinated by these songs when she heard of them from some old women in the poorhouse; she told Yeats and Douglas Hyde about them; Hyde helped to found the Gaelic League; the new political generation 'went to school' with the Gaelic League; politics and culture combined to fuel the War of Independence; the War of Independence led to the setting up of the Irish Free State; *ergo*, Raiftearaí was responsible for the political freedom gained in 1922.

Crude and simplistic when put as baldly as that, but possessing large smidgens of truth nonetheless.

There was a rapprochment between all the forces of cultural and political nationalism from the 1880s to the 1920s and this fed into a powerful revival that changed the nature of Irish society until the present time.

An obvious example is the Gaelic Athletic Association. Organised sport was only beginning to grow for the masses in the second half of the nineteenth century in any country in Europe. Previous to this it was the preserve of the huntin' shootin' fishin' leisured aristocracy. Sport did exist, of course, but it was usually uncodified, crude and dangerous. After the famine, the growth of bourgeois respectability managed to put an end to bull-baiting, cock-fighting (nearly) and bare-knuckle brawling. The ancient game of hurling almost suffered the same fate as in some areas of the country it was hardly distinguishable from faction fighting. It survived because it had the skeleton of an organised structure, partly deriving from the time when landlords arranged games between their tenants in the eighteenth century, and partly from an embryonic structure of clubs in places like Cork. The game was wiped out in large tracts of the country, but survived in those areas of greatest skill where the local passions were strongest and an appreciation of its artistry was most felt.

This might not have happened, however, were it not for the genius of Michael Cusack (1847–1906) whose vision, determination, and singlemindedness helped put the GAA on a solid basis. The crude caricature of him as the Citizen in Joyce's *Ulysses* is unfair in its depiction and inaccurate in point of fact, but remains a powerful piece of fanciful invention. The GAA was also lucky to benefit from the politics of other sports who were aligned with the establishment and whose Sabbatarianism did not allow people to enjoy themselves on a Sunday. As that day was the only day of rest for most ordinary Catholics they flocked to Gaelic games for their leisure activities.

The growth of the GAA is one of the most remarkable success stories of the cultural revival. It need not have been so. Ireland is almost unique in Europe in having native field games that are far more popular than the international ball games of soccer and rugby. As early as the first decade of the century more than 20,000 were attending big games. All the best stadiums in the country belong to the GAA. The principal stadium of Croke Park will fill up with 60,000 people several times each year, although it once took more than 90,000 when Down reached the all-Ireland final for the first time in 1961. This was an amazing leap forward for a game that was an uncodified scramble for a pig's bladder between contending parishes less than a century before.

The main reasons these games are the most popular in the country are that they are the most thrilling when played at their best. They are simply more exciting. Gaelic football combines the skill of soccer with the physical contact of rugby and the swiftness of Australian rules. They also benefit because they reflect, particularly at local level, genuine regional loyalties of deep and dark passion. And even though the counties are an English administrative invention, they often sufficiently match older Gaelic polities for battles long ago to be re-enacted on the field of play. In fact, the GAA has moulded regional identity along county lines in a way that is quite new while appearing to be of time immemorial.

When two Irish people meet abroad the first question they are likely to ask is 'Where are you from?' People mark themselves not so much by class or by occupation but by their regional loyalties. The reply to that question is often measured in terms of the success of the county hurling or football team. It is also a conversation opener or stopper depending on place and interest. It provides endless banter and repartee, and is one of the great bonding agents of Irish life. The GAA may also have been responsible for bringing the very word 'Gaelic' back into common usage and giving it a positive gloss.

The Irish literary revival had a very intimate relationship with Gaelic Ireland. The great writers of the 1880–1920 period, whose names are internationally known, were consciously part of a literary movement whose aim it was to give Ireland back to itself. A crude but not inaccurate summing-up of their creed might be that they sought to mend the broken Irish tradition and to render it into English. Nationalist literature is caught in the dilemma that it is simultaneously trying to be a continuation of the old and a creator of the unimagined new. But the attempts were great. Yeats immersed himself in Irish mythology and smelt fairies where none had been smelt before; Lady Gregory reinterpreted the Irish sagas; John Millington Synge went to the Aran Islands and invented a dialect of exotic idioms and poetic flourishes which he claimed was based on Irish; Seán O'Casey was a member of the Gaelic League; George Moore allowed a book of his stories to be published first in Irish before the English version; even Oscar Wilde's fairy stories are redolent of the Irish folk tales which he must have heard from his mother who was an ardent enthusiast for Gaelic Ireland.

But others were having none of this.

The idea of an Ireland without the Irish language may have been anathema to only a small minority in the 1880s, but the idea of the nation expressing itself entirely through English and at the same time maintaining its identity was to them intellectually dishonest. The Gaelic League (*Conradh na Gaeilge*) was founded in 1893 with the aim of supporting and strengthening the Irish language as a spoken tongue, and of developing a modern literature. In this it was quite distinct from previous organisations whose purpose was generally antiquarian or learned. It rapidly proved to be a revolutionary organisation with a quickening and developing philosophy. This philosophy may be said to have begun with a famous lecture by Douglas Hyde 'On the necessity for de-Anglicising Ireland' to the National Literary Society in 1892 and to grow eventually into a fully revivalist one over the following years. The League set up branches throughout the country and had as many as 600 by 1908. They organised language classes and social gatherings and entertainments. They sent teachers from parish to parish to bring the language back to those areas that had only abandoned it a generation or two previously. They set up a publishing house and a very successful newspaper. They involved themselves in public campaigns to have Irish accepted as an obligatory subject for the matriculation examination of the new National University of Ireland, and were successful because they had popular local political support. They supported Irish industry and goods and were hugely involved in urging that St Patrick's Day be declared a national holiday.

It was an organisation dedicated to cultural nationalism with the language at its centre. In this model culture is being summoned to play the role that politics would normally do. It must unify and salve and promote, but at the same time remain quiescent. The Gaelic League was determinedly non-political at first. Douglas Hyde, by his idealism, gentle persuasion and unquestioning probity, had managed to bring people from all classes and backgrounds into the movement. He was correct in seeing the danger of politics but was naive in thinking it could be avoided. Cultural nationalism does not always lead to a political direction, but under certain conditions it is inevitable. We might say that the Gaelic League was infiltrated by the revolutionary IRB (Irish Republican Brotherhood), or that the IRB was infiltrated by the Gaelic League. The Irish political, cultural, language, literary and sporting revolution was all of a piece, and drew much of its inspiration from its Gaelic past.

THE NEW STATE

It is not surprising therefore that, from the beginning and for some time after, much of the symbolism of the new Irish state in the 26 counties of the country should invoke that Gaelic past. The harp that sits on Government documentation might be that which once thrummed through Tara's halls. The Irish parliament is the *Dáil*. The chairman of proceedings is the *Ceann Comhairle*. The chief minister and head of the government is *An Taoiseach*; the deputy head, *An Tánaiste*. The elected representatives are *Teachtaí Dála* (TDs). The upper house *Seanad Éireann*. The two houses and the President are collectively *An tOireachtas*. And while this may seem like fancy plumage, the first Dáil of January 1919 was conducted largely in Irish. This may have been partly a show of nationalist separatism and cultural independence, but many TDs were serious about turning the machinery of the new state into a totally Irish one.

That they did not was due to the death of idealism in the wake of the civil war (1922–3), the sheer difficulty of getting the state up and running materially, and the simplistic understanding of how language and cultural change comes about. It took 300 years of unrelenting attrition to bring the Irish language to its knees, and government ministers believed that by teaching it in schools the process would be reversed within a generation. There was certainly great enthusiasm within the education system itself. Teachers flocked to summer colleges where they learned the language as adequately as they could, while the language became compulsory for all children attending schools. Infant classes were taught through Irish in the belief that it would expand and grow throughout the education system, which in many ways it did.

The government founded and funded a state publishing house known as *An Gúm* in 1926 whose purpose was to produce Irish-language textbooks and reading material. It ran a very imaginative translation service whereby authors were paid to Irishify novels, stories and plays in the belief that you cannot summon authors up from nowhere ready-made, but you may train translators rather more quickly. Many of the world's classics emanated from this publishing house over the following 20 years including works by Dickens, Tolstoy, Moliére and Shakespeare. Because many of the very best Irish authors were involved in this scheme the quality of the writing is often far superior to the original work of the same period.

The government also established the Irish Folklore

Commission in 1935 to collect, store and study what remained of the popular culture of the rural poor. They were so successful that they now have the largest collection of folklore in the world. The study of folklore was seen as a vital adjunct to the language itself, since Irish only now survived as a first language in scattered communities mostly along the western seaboard.

This fascination with folklore had its positive and negative sides. The recording and saving of stories and songs is a contribution to the spiritual enrichment of humankind. The act of listening and saving in itself added dignity to the lives of many storytellers who thought their art was despised and forgotten. Collectors tell of informants who were positively excited and ennobled by the prospect of the riches of their minds being preserved for ever. And some of these storytellers were prodigious. Seán Ó Conaill (1835–1931) from west Kerry gave the scholar Séamus Ó Duilearga enough material for a book of 500 pages of dense print. He had never been to school, knew no English and never left his native district, yet retained inside his head a massive store of oral culture that had been handed down from generation to generation.

Nobody knows how old most of these stories are, although some very few can be traced to a literary original. Some are part of a bigger network of tales that stretch in lines of memory around the globe. Others are versions of long sagas that could take several nights to narrate. And yet more reflect a belief in the pagan Otherworld that should have been buried underneath the bell, book and candle of 1500 years of Christianity.

There is a tale of a young girl who is brought to a fairy birth in a fairy palace in a fairy hill. When the baby is born it is immediatley chucked into a fire and burned. All of the many people at the birth stick their fingers in the ashes of the baby and rub it on their eyes. The girl does the same on one of her eyes. Some time later she meets a man at a fair and greets him. He expresses surprise that she sees him, because he is one of the fairy folk.

'How do you see me?' he asks her.

'With this eye,' she says, pointing to the eye on which she rubbed the ashes.

'Then you will see me no more,' he said, and shoved his finger into the socket and plucked out her eye.

The story illustrates the nature of the Irish Otherworld which lives side by side with our own. The girl had been given the gift of second sight which allowed her see the two worlds simultaneously. This Otherworld is not somewhere to go to after death as in Christianity, but is here beside us all the time like another dimension. Underneath the official story of the Irish people this folk culture survived, a curious mix of the pagan and the pious, the sane and the superstitious, like all cultures.

For the city folk who visited these rural outposts, the *Gaeltacht* was a balm from the grinding mills of the big town and a flight from modernity. Even those from the Gaeltacht itself often internalised this vision. The great storyteller Peig Sayers (1873–1958) once remarked that she had lived on the Great Blasket for most of her life and had never heard a cross word spoken amongst the people there. One of the more prominent modern Irish poets, Máirtín Ó Direáin (1910–1988), made a career of romanticising the Aran Islands which he had safely left and moaning about the awful city in which he made his living. Liam O'Flaherty, also from the Aran Islands, and who wrote in both English and Irish, has a doctor character in his fine novel *Skerret* remark, 'All this new education and new habits of life that are being introduced into this island are only breaking up the peace and happiness of the people,' and he continues to wax poetically about the rural commune and how the country folk helped one another. This local organic community lived in an undisturbed time-bubble from which the city corrupted could draw sustenance. It was little wonder that there was a certain confusion between Gaelic culture and agriculture (of the ekeing-out-a-living sort).

But this folk culture also had its sinister side. Apart from the belief that the language itself was only fit for discussions of the most sublimely poetic or the utterly rural – Anthony Burgess remarked that his efforts to learn Irish always faltered when he came to a sentence such as 'The priest has tied a string to the left crubeen of the pig' – there was nothing either truly romantic or idyllically cooperative about the country. Much religious or proto-religious belief is deeply metaphoric, but when it clashes with the literal it can have disturbing results. The tragedy of Bridget Cleary who was burned to death by her husband and relatives in 1895 in the sincere belief that she was a changeling left by the fairies is a case in point. Folk tradition is replete with the boycotting of people whose ideas do not concur with those of the community, with abductions and kidnappings, child murders, maimings and woundings, malicious burnings. There are stories of old people being banished from their homes or put to death by smothering on reaching a certain age. The eminent folklorist Seán Ó Súilleabháin produced his *Handbook of Irish Folklore* as a guide to collectors in the field; amongst hundreds of questions and leads he asks his workers to be on the look-out for the kinds of punishments meted out to those condemned by local opinion: they were to be aware of punishment by burning, covering with tar and feathers, nails, hair or beard pulled off, tongue or eyes or ears cut out, maiming, flaying, skinning, exposure to death by drowning, hunger, cold or heat, being torn between two horses ...

The confusion between the Gaeltacht as the source of the language *or* as a way of life bedevilled the public debate for decades. The Gaeltacht itself was continuing to decline as a result of the historical momentum built up over the previous century, and because of emigration and language change. And yet, when the Swiss linguist and scholar Heinrich Wagner toured the country in the late 1940s through to the mid-1950s gathering material for his *Linguistic Atlas and Survey of Irish Dialects* he discovered Irish speakers in counties and in corners of counties which are not now included in the Gaeltacht. These included counties Louth and Kilkenny in Leinster, Tipperary and Clare in Munster, Sligo and Leitrim in Connacht, and Cavan, Monaghan, Antrim and Tyrone in Ulster. Although the present Gaeltacht is confined to about 30,000 speakers in Donegal, Galway and Kerry with smaller communities of some hundreds in Cork, Waterford, Mayo and Meath there is no doubt that the rate of decline has slowed down. This is partly due to increased prosperity and the halt of emigration, but also to a pride in their definition of themselves as Irish-speaking communities. New institutions which have been set up in the Gaeltacht, particularly the nation-wide Raidió na Gaeltachta and television service Teilifís na Gaeilge, have given this self-confidence a boost. Those searching for fireside tales as a communal activity will find the TV in the corner; and the dancing at the crossroads of much mocking merriment has long been replaced by the disco with all gyrations and transactions performed in the native language.

But the old can also live alongside the new. One of the greatest revolutions in Irish culture has been the growth in the popularity of Irish music. The Irish céilí bands of the 1920s and '30s were usually an ensemble of two piano accordions drowning out a regularity of fiddles and flutes. To the untutored ear they reeled away with endless monotony. One of the mysteries of the universe was how they all managed to stop together. Irish songs would at best be patriotic ballads, but far more usually some weepy emigrant song which came filtered through the music hall.

Radio request programmes featured 'How can I buy Killarney?', or 'If we only had old Ireland over here', or 'McNamara's band' as Irish music. The real genuine stuff had not yet been allowed to come out to play.

Some of the credit for this must initially go to the ballad boom of the 1960s. The Clancy Brothers and Tommy Makem had enough commercial savvy to milk the American market with a clever mix of nationalism, sentimentality, wit and more importantly, the real thing. Like The Dubliners who came along about the same time, they were real musicians. While part of the growing international folk scene, they were also Irish down to the deeps. They were part of the softening-up process for what was to come next.

Although Seán Ó Riada (1931–1971) was already known from the score of the films *Mise Éire* (1959) and *Saoirse* (1961), it was his work with the talented group of musicians who became known as Ceoltóirí Chualann that revolutionised Irish music. In the first instance he plundered the tradition for tunes that had been long forgotten. He introduced instruments that had been banished from the céilí band, including the classy harpsichord and the humble bodhrán. He gave pride of place to the uillean pipes and allowed the musicians to play now together, then singly, and then again in varied combination. They gave sell-out concerts to large theatres in the late 1960s when a few years previously they would not have half-filled a dingy parish hall. Ó Riada himself theorised endlessly and popularised his revolution by lectures, radio and television. He argued that Irish music was essentially outside the mainstream Italo-Germanic tradition and had much in common with the European periphery.

This was a theory also supported by the film-maker Bob Quinn who became fascinated by the style of singing known as *sean-nós* (old style) which he encountered when he went to live in the Connemara Gaeltacht. In a series of TV films he contended that Irish singing was more akin to what we hear in Eastern Europe or amongst the Tatars or the Arabs than other European folk traditions. He didn't quite go so far as to argue that the Irish were really Arabs, but he rubbished the Celtic origins to his own satisfaction. His idea that cultural traditions travel more easily by sea than by land is eminently sensible, and there is nothing implausible about his own or Ó Riada's theories about Irish music.

The *sean-nós* singing which fascinated them both is exotic to the unpractised ear, but perfectly normal to those whom it surrounds. It is an unaccompanied style of singing where the performer can vary the pace and rhythm of his song according to time or occasion or mood or audience. Although apparently decorated by gracenotes which slide up and down syllables and which can linger on consonants in hugging embrace, the tune itself is always the central scaffolding of the song. Despised as a relic of poverty for so long it has in recent years become quite fashionable, with more popular groups featuring *sean-nós* singers at their concerts. In another time and another place Darach Ó Catháin might have been a great blues performer as his every word breathes soul and passion, while a younger singer like Iarla Ó Lionáird is willing to mix his traditional repertoire with the best of contemporary world music.

Gaelic culture is there to serve the country and the people like anything else that is humanly made. It is not a static artefact in a preserved tongue which cannot change or grow. It will, inevitably, be caught between the keepers of the true flame and the purveyors of kitsch. The *Riverdance* phenomenon, for example, burst the restricting bonds of Irish dance for ever. It gave dancers back their hands and released the beauty of the whole body. But it wasn't as new as it seemed. Much traditional

Irish dance allowed the use of the hands and the shoulders in free rhythmic expressions on the flagstones of the kitchen floor. When Irish dance became regularised and systematised under the influence of the great cultural festival of the Oireachtas (1897) in the late nineteenth century, it became confined with the straightjacket of Victorian stuffiness. Legs were in but only from the knees down and hands were kept firmly in place on both sides of the body in a form of rigor mortis. They were also highly useful in holding flowing kilts and skirts from rising beyond their station. Apart from music, traditional dance was the most widely disseminated art form throughout the Irish diaspora in the twentieth century. Although the dress code was often Celtic kitsch, and the accompanying music clanging and repetitive, the ankles were always well-turned, the toe well-tapped, and the kick forever below the waist. As against the sincerity of generations of young Irish children at home and abroad sweating in dingy parish halls until their number was proclaimed, *Riverdance* and *Lord of the Dance* exposed the dangers of what is often called crass commercial exploitation. Art must live on the edge of the precipice and take its chances or die; but it may fall over anyway.

NOW AND IN TIME TO COME

The matter of Ireland is the favourite discourse of the Irish intelligentsia. This is so because the country was thoroughly colonised, and yet survived. Anglicised, but not completely. Gained independence, but not for everyone. Full of bravado, but beset with nagging doubts. The Irish are still an enigma to themselves, and are in a constant scramble of self-discovery.

The Irish language was not revived – although 'restoration' is a more suitable word since it never died – as the leaders of the cultural revolution wished, but it is equally certain that it will not depart the scene and go the way of Manx or Cornish. There will always be communities or networks of Irish speakers in the country, whether large or small. There will always be public support, both hot and cold; and state support, either vigorous or light. The fact that Gaelic culture will not go away means that Ireland will always have to deal with it, lying as it does both underneath its common forms and beside them simultaneously. There is a strange pattern of bilingualism and usage in the country which ranges from the Gaeltacht resident for whom it is the first and mother and everyday tongue to the person with what is colloquially known as the *cúpla focal* or 'two words'. In between there is a speckled and macular picture of partial usage amongst the 40 per cent of the population who claim to know some of the language. Networks of Irish speakers effectively create a Gaeltacht of common interest. This is a helpful way to think about them, as the original meaning of the word Gaeltacht meant something like 'the Irishry', or those who spoke Irish and/or associated with it. The geographical meaning is unnecessarily limiting. These networks operate through Irish-medium schools, or artistic events, or festivals, or occasions, or organisations, or interests. They are fed by their own dynamic and by the passive sympathy of most of the population. Not a restoration in the full-blooded sense, but not merely a minority language either.

Nevertheless there is a sense in which the language has been restored. The twentieth century has seen it reclaim itself as a full language of usage rather than as a despised gibberish of the deserving poor scattered into mutually unintelligible dialects out on the farthest reaches of the land. It has worked its way back into those domains from which it was banished since the seventeenth century. It has been extended in several senses of that word. There is now real institutional support of a kind undreamt of 100 years ago – including an all-Ireland cross-border body, *Bord na Gaeilge/An Foras Teanga,* for its promotion, and a government ministry. It is used in radio, television, film and print journalism. It has been fashioned for use in all the high registers of language – law, administration, science, scholarship. It has been hammered into a standard form which is now widely accepted. Academies exist for its study and its shaping. New dialects have emerged amongst learners that are proving tough and independent – and new dialects are always a sign of real life. It is available as a national language if the people decide they require it.

The Irish literature of the twentieth century has been richer and more plentiful than any previous century. In the first instance this is a question of volume. There is simply more Irish writing and more Irish books in the last hundred years than in all the previous centuries put together. If more does not necessarily mean better it certainly means enough. There has been enough literature composed since 1910 – especially novels, stories and poetry – to say that the Gaelic League's 1893 aim of promoting a modern literature has been a resounding success. Works of scholarship have contributed significantly to Irish intellectual knowledge, and several books have fundamentally rewritten our understanding of ourselves.

There is also the paradox that the very strength of English, which once was the engine that sucked the language dry, may now be of some assistance in its support. English has moved from being just a language of conquest to being *the* major world language at the present time, and for the foreseeable future as long as the United States rules the air. Crude as it may seem, most other languages are simply not needed when it comes to commerce and business and communications and the stuff of international palaver. From now on, the main reason for learning languages will be cultural. And from a cultural point of view the most important language for the Irish must needs be their own. Because of American influence and dominance sweeping all before it, there is a far greater understanding of the importance of 'native' cultures. Multiculturalism implies just that, a multiplicity of cultures.

Gaelic culture and the Irish language are both very real and very symbolic. And the symbol is the compliment that the actual pays to the ideal. At a very deep level the country knows where it has come from. The shoddiest craftshop, the most wonderful *fleádh ceoil*, the three-chord balladeer, the epenthetic vowel, the most skilful hurling match between Cork and Offaly, ogham pennants, Aran sweaters, souvenir Claddagh rings, the Irish pub, leprechaun cabarets, kinds of stained-glass windows, loquacious silence, Celtic cross headstones, the fiddling at Doolin, *ceol agus craic*, the formalisation of informality, medieval banquets, and whatever long list makes Ireland distinctive all owe something to the Gaelic tradition. It is not just the ghost at the feast but the very shape of the room we live in.

A POCKET HISTORY OF IRELAND
Breandán Ó hEithir

Concise, insightful overview of Ireland's history from Celtic times to the present, including the North of Ireland. Illustrated.

Paperback £4.99/$7.95/€6.34

A POCKET HISTORY OF IRISH LITERATURE
A. Norman Jeffares

Traces the long list of Irish writers, from Swift to writers of the twenty-first century: Synge, O'Casey, Beckett, Joyce, Julia O'Faolain, Paul Durcan, Kate O'Brien, Roddy Doyle, Seamus Heaney ...

Paperback £4.99/$7.95/€6.34

A POCKET HISTORY OF IRISH TRADITIONAL MUSIC
Gearóid Ó hAllmhuráin

The history of Irish traditional music, song and dance from the mythological harp of the Dagda right up to Riverdance.

Paperback £4.99/$7.95/€6.34

A POCKET HISTORY OF IRISH REBELS
Morgan Llewelyn

The rebel has always played an important role in Irish history. This book describes the life and times of the most famous, and the most infamous: Thomas FitzGerald, Granuaile, Dónal O'Sullivan Beare, Owen Roe O'Neill, Theobald Wolfe Tone, Father John Murphy, Robert Emmet, Daniel O'Connell, William Smith O'Brien, John Mitchel, James Connolly, Constance Markievicz, James Larkin, Patrick Pearse, Terence MacSwiney, Michael Collins, Bobby Sands, Gerry Adams.

Paperback £4.99/$7.95/€6.34

Send for our full colour catalogue

A POCKET BOOK OF THE BANSHEE

Patricia Lysaght

The Banshee, or messenger of death, has been in Irish myths for centuries and forms the basis for many Irish ghost stories. Never seen, her unearthly wailing has been heard by many.

Paperback £4.99/$7.95/€6.34

A POCKET HISTORY OF THE IRA

Brendan O'Brien

Updated in 2000, this is the story of the IRA from its foundation to today, tracing the changes and developments that have influenced the organisation and the varying political environments in which it has operated.

Paperback £4.99/$7.95/€6.34

A POCKET HISTORY OF ULSTER

Brian Barton

Unravels the complicated origins and course of Northern Irish history in a straightforward, accessible text. Illustrated.

Paperback £5.99/$7.95/€7.61